Reflecting Theologically on AIDS

Reflecting Theologically on AIDS

A Global Challenge

Edited by
Robin Gill

scm press

British Library Cataloguing in Publication data

A catalogue record for this book is available
from the British Library

978-0-334-04002-6

First published in 2007 by SCM Press
9–17 St Alban's Place,
London N1 0NX

www.scm-canterburypress.co.uk

SCM Press is a division of
SCM-Canterbury Press Ltd

Typeset by Regent Typesetting, London
Printed and bound in Great Britain by
William Clowes Ltd, Beccles, Suffolk

Contents

Acknowledgements

I would particularly like to thank all of the participants in the Windhoek workshop for prompting and inspiring this book. Calle Almedal of UNAIDS was the driving force behind this workshop. He had the vision to see that faith groups can make an important contribution to changing attitudes globally towards those living with AIDS and to helping to stop the spread of the HIV virus. At the workshop itself Gillian Paterson of Paxworks UK worked tirelessly on draft after draft of the Windhoek Report which is reproduced here and even persuaded me to do some drafting while other participants slept! Robert Vitillo, as mentioned in the Introduction, offered invaluable help in putting this book together. I am also most grateful to Barbara Laing of SCM Press for her enthusiastic support for this project. Finally, as ever, my love to Jenny and to our three grandchildren. By the grace of God may theirs be a world without AIDS.

Robin Gill
The Feast of the Transfiguration, 2006

UNHCR UNODC
UNICEF ILO
WFP UNESCO
UNDP WHO
UNFPA WORLD BANK

JOINT UNITED NATIONS PROGRAMME ON HIV/AIDS

The Contributors

Denise M. Ackermann is Professor of Theology at the University of Stellenbosch and was a member of the Windhoek workshop.

Lisa Sowle Cahill is J. Donald Monan, SJ, Professor of Theology at Boston College.

Musa W. Dube is Professor of New Testament at the University of Botswana and was a member of the Windhoek workshop.

Margaret A. Farley is the Gilbert L. Stark Professor of Christian Ethics at Yale University Divinity School.

Robin Gill is Michael Ramsey Professor of Modern Theology at the University of Kent, Canterbury, and was a member of the Windhoek workshop.

James F. Keenan is Professor of Moral Theology at the Weston Jesuit School of Theology in Cambridge, Massachusetts.

Enda McDonagh is Emeritus Professor of Theology at St Patrick's College, Maynooth, and was a member of the Windhoek workshop.

Leonard M. Martin was, until his death, Professor of Ethics at the State University of Ceará, Fortaleza, Brazil, and was a member of the Windhoek workshop.

Gareth Moore was, until his death, Lecturer in Philosophy at Blackfriars, Oxford.

Stan Nussbaum researches for Global Mapping International, Colorado Springs.

The Contributors

Charles Ryan is Lecturer at St Joseph's Theological Institute, Cedara, South Africa.

Robert J. Vitillo works for Caritas Internationalis in Geneva.

Gunther H. Wittenberg is Emeritus Professor of Old Testament Studies, School of Theology, University of Natal.

Introduction

In December 2003 UNAIDS, the Joint United Nations Programme on HIV and AIDS, supported a workshop of Christian theologians at Windhoek, Namibia. We were encouraged to produce a framework for theological reflection addressing the challenge of AIDS. UNAIDS was of course fully aware both of rates of HIV inflection that are dramatically increasing in many countries around the world, and in particular those in Sub-Saharan Africa, and of the devastation caused by AIDS disease, especially among the poor. UNAIDS emphatically did not need academic theologians to do epidemiology. What UNAIDS wanted was theological reflection, explicitly stating that it 'recognizes and values the efforts carried out by religious groups in care and treatment of people living with HIV infection and AIDS'.[1]

The Windhoek Report that emerged from the workshop is reproduced as Chapter 1 of this book, 'HIV- and AIDS-Related Stigma'. One of the more remarkable features of the workshop was that about half of the 62 theologians present were Catholics. It soon became obvious that in practical terms the Catholic Church, principally through the work of Caritas Internationalis, has responded to the challenge of AIDS more energetically than most other Christian bodies. Yet ironically the Catholic Church has also been criticized more heavily than others by secular agencies. The work of Caritas Internationalis is too often ignored by secular commentators.

Reflecting Theologically on AIDS is an attempt to bring the theological reflection that is developing in both the Catholic

---

1 UNAIDS, February 2005, *A Report of a Theological Workshop Focusing on HIV- and AIDS-Related Stigma*, p. 2: http://www.unaids.org.

and non-Catholic churches to a wider academic audience. Some of the chapters have never been published before, and others have appeared only in journals and books with small readerships. The book arises from my own conviction, fired by the Windhoek workshop, that there does need to be wider and deeper theological reflection about the challenge of AIDS today. It is too easy for those in the Northern Hemisphere to treat AIDS as a distant problem. Reflecting theologically at Windhoek with Christians living with HIV was a transforming experience. AIDS is a challenge for the whole Church. It needs more theological attention than it has received so far. If this book helps even a little to give it that attention then it will have achieved its purpose.

Father Robert J. Vitillo MSW of Caritas Internationalis was immensely helpful in identifying some of the theological essays that might be included in the book. His previously unpublished essay 'The Human and Pastoral Challenges of HIV and AIDS' is Chapter 2. He outlines some of the main features of the HIV and AIDS crisis – power inequalities, poverty, sexual abuse, stigmatization and marginalization – and relates them to action that the Church has already, or has not yet, made. For Vitillo the issue of justice is crucial to an adequate theological response to the challenge of AIDS.

Writing from his long experience in Zambia the Jesuit theologian Michael J. Kelly has identified the following ways in which churches have responded to this challenge:

- Their strong human rights based approach that promotes a culture of life, respect for the sacredness of the individual and the celebration of life.
- The enormous efforts that they pour into care for the infected and impact mitigation for the affected – religious bodies provide between a quarter and a half of all the AIDS care in the world. Care, support and treatment are integral to prevention, creating a more effective environment for it.
- Christian social teaching that advocates strongly for the transformation of economic, political and social structures that effectively exclude the poor and deny the equal personal role and dignity of women. In other words, fundamental

church teaching consistently and effectively addresses some of the major driving forces of the AIDS epidemic.

- The concern of religious organizations to promote a strong sense of community and social cohesion among their members – the degree of such cohesion has been identified as being a key factor determining the speed with which HIV infection spreads and the numbers who become infected.
- The immediate contact that religious personnel maintain with people at the grassroots level. They deal with them directly, in their homes and elsewhere, without recourse to other intermediary functionaries. UNAIDS has stressed how grassroots and community mobilization is the core strategy on which success against HIV/AIDS builds.
- The high moral standards promoted by the churches. The Catholic Church is resolute in proposing high ideals for its members and in requiring sexual abstinence outside marriage, the only completely certain way of avoiding the sexual transmission of HIV. It is equally resolute in requiring fidelity within marriage, which – apart from the case of a discordant couple – is the only completely sure way of not becoming HIV infected when practising sex. In maintaining these ideals, the Church is adopting a prophetic stance against the debasing of the body and the commodification of women and girls, and in favour of the institution of the family.[2]

Like Vitillo, Kelly is committed to the central concept of justice and is aware that churches could still be doing more than they are at present. Helpfully he identifies three key functions for churches – as servant, as teacher and as prophet:

> As *servant*, the Church must face the challenges of stigma and discrimination that poison human relationships, bring enormous personal pain to those who experience these, and make it very difficult to bring the disease out into the open so that it can be both checked and treated. The Church must also ensure that it incorporates people living with HIV and/or

---

2 Michael J. Kelly SJ, April 2006, *HIV and AIDS: A Justice Perspective*, p. 59, Jesuit Centre for Theological Reflection, 10101 Lusaka, Zambia: http://www.jctr.org.zm.

AIDS into its life and practices, establishing solidarity with them, making them welcome as integral and valuable members of the community, and making it possible for them to participate in real and meaningful ways in church and community life . . . As *teacher*, the Church is challenged to deal more openly and positively with sexuality, not seeing this as something undesirable or even wrong, but developing a theology that acknowledges the goodness of sexuality and recognizes its role in human development and happiness. This also calls for a more developed morality that is no longer excessively concerned with rules and prescriptions but seeks to build up an understanding of the human conscience as the bulwark of moral understanding and behaviour and that liberates individuals to exercise personal responsibility in their lives . . . As *prophet*, the Church is challenged to show itself as a leader in the struggle with the epidemic. This means it must bring its wisdom, resources and advocacy to bear on all aspects – prevention, care, support, treatment, orphan care, stigma, human rights abuses, female disempowerment, poverty, exploitative socio-economic structures and practices, and the mitigation of negative impacts. The Church's leadership role would be enhanced if it acknowledged publicly that its own members (religious personnel, ministers and lay persons) have AIDS so that it could be seen to be speaking and leading from a position of strength, internal knowledge and understanding, arising from an awareness of its own infection.[3]

Chapter 3, by the veteran Catholic theologian Professor Enda McDonagh of St Patrick's College, Maynooth, was originally published in the *Irish Theological Quarterly* in 1994 (60:2, pp. 81–99). McDonagh is the author of a number of important theological books, including *Invitation and Response: Essays in Christian Moral Theology* (1972), *Gift and Call* (1975) and *Doing the Truth* (1979), all published in Dublin by Gill & Macmillan. Like Vitillo he was also a participant at the Windhoek workshop. In this essay he identifies the Synoptic

---

3 Kelly, *HIV and AIDS*, p. 61.

Jesus' values of the Kingdom of God as being particularly important for theology in a time of AIDS. These values are based upon 'effective love, feeding the hungry, setting the prisoners free, restoring sight to the blind, letting the lame walk, healing all manner of sickness'. They are also concerned with 'truth' – a casualty all too often of the AIDS pandemic – with justice, with 'peace' (*shalom*), with companionship and with care.

The fourth and fifth chapters are also by Catholic theologians, both of whom focus upon the importance of 'responsibility' as a theological response to the challenge of AIDS. Father Charles Ryan is a priest in the Archdiocese of Durban, South Africa, and Lecturer at St Joseph's Theological Institute, Cedara. His essay was first published in 2003 in Stuart C. Bate (ed.), *Responsibility in a Time of AIDS: A Pastoral Response by Catholic Theologians and AIDS Activists in Southern Africa* (Catholic Theological Society of Southern Africa, Cluster Publications). Ryan raises important theological questions about theodicy (is God really responsible for AIDS?), about individual responsibility and about the responsibility of the Church in South Africa in the presence of AIDS. In the process he highlights issues that are just as appropriate for many other countries – especially the gap between popular perceptions of sexuality and official church teaching on the subject. He also raises bluntly the prudential consideration that 'the technical reality is that sex with a condom is safer than sex without a condom – all other things being equal'. The issue of condoms soon introduced divisions among the theologians at Windhoek – with unexpected allegiances between Catholics and non-Catholics for and against their prudential use in the context of HIV infection.

The Dominican theologian and Lecturer in Philosophy at Blackfriars, Oxford, the late Gareth Moore, was also well aware of such tensions. This fifth chapter was originally published in 1990 in a special edition on 'Christians and AIDS' in *New Blackfriars* (71:840, July/August 1990, pp. 334–42).[4] In

---

4 For an Orthodox approach at the time see Basil Zion's 'The Orthodox Church and the AIDS Crisis', *St Vladimir's Theological Quarterly* 36:1–2, pp. 152–8, republished in Kenneth R. Overberg SF (ed.), 1994, *AIDS, Ethics and Religion: Embracing a World of Suffering*, Maryknoll, NY: Orbis, pp. 243–8.

the late 1980s the Dominicans at Blackfriars became particularly active in responding to the challenge of AIDS. Under the leadership of Father Timothy Radcliffe they became both advocates and carers at a time when AIDS was primarily associated with the gay community. This is reflected in the opening paragraph of Moore's essay. It is of course recognized now that HIV infection globally has more to do with heterosexual activity. It was tempting on this account not to include this essay. However, I think that would have been unfortunate. Moore's essay raises many important theological considerations that are still relevant and it is fitting to remember the pioneer work of the Oxford Dominicans in the late 1980s. In their Preface to the special edition of *New Blackfriars* the Dominicans John Orme Mills and Antoine Lion argue for greater 'generosity and compassion' when faced with criticism for devoting a whole edition to this issue. They insist:

> Christians are concerned when sexuality, the seat of life, has become a possible place of death; when many, both the young and (now more often) the not so young, seem still to be unaware that certain practices put their lives in danger; when so many people, struck at the deepest level, must rediscover their whole way of life; when the sick or those close to them are on a road of suffering and often seek in vain for comfort; when irrational fears circulate and, to the physical and psychological trials caused by the virus itself, add the experience of being discarded and judged by a part of society. The Churches are themselves touched when certain of their members enter this way of suffering; Christians, confronted by AIDS, may not enjoy at a distance some divine immunity.[5]

Few, if any, other British theological journals at the time had the courage and foresight to devote a whole edition to the challenge of AIDS. The Anglican editor of *Theology*, the late Peter Coleman, did write an editorial in May 1988 on 'AIDS – A Serious Threat and a New Opportunity'.[6] His book *Gay*

---

5 John Orme Mills and Antoine Lion, 'Preface', *New Blackfriars* 71:840, July/August 1990, p. 319.
6 *Theology* XCI:741, pp. 171–3.

Christians: A Moral Dilemma published the following year by SCM Press, also sought to promote a tolerant and irenic attitude to homosexuality within churches (albeit an attitude that did not survive the 1998 Lambeth Conference of Anglican Bishops[7] – a conference that he attended as an observer after his retirement). Yet little else in *Theology* at the time or since has been concerned with the theological challenge of AIDS.

If the initial contributors here are Catholic theologians (recognizing the importance of the Catholic response to the challenge of AIDS) the next few are not. However, like Robert Vitillo and Enda McDonagh, Musa Dube, Denise Ackermann and myself were all participants at the Windhoek workshop. Dube and Ackermann were both lecturers at this, and Ackermann's lecture is the chapter reproduced here. Dube, Ackermann and myself also have a common aim – to engage directly in theological education on the challenge of AIDS, using the Bible as our primary resource.

Musa W. Dube is Professor of New Testament at the University of Botswana and also seconded to the World Council of Churches as HIV and AIDS theological consultant. She is editor of *HIV/AIDS and the Curriculum: Methods of Integrating HIV/AIDS in Theological Programmes* from which Chapter 6 is abstracted (pp. 48–56). In the Introduction she writes that the book as a whole 'represents our efforts in the continent of Africa to contribute towards the struggle against HIV/AIDS'.[8] She sees this as a necessary redress:

> In response to the urgent needs of the moment, it became clear that the answer to the question, 'Is religion part of the problem?' was yes. This took many forms. It included silence

---

7 It is worth noting that in the 1988 Lambeth Conference Reports, 35 paragraphs were given to the challenge of AIDS and just three to homosexuality (see The Anglican Consultative Council, 1988, *The Truth Shall Make You Free: The Lambeth Conference 1988: The Reports, Resolutions and Pastoral Letterrs from the Bishops*, London, pp. 188ff.) but in the 1998 Lambeth Conference Reports homosexuality alone became the issue.

8 Musa W. Dube, 2003, *HIV/AIDS and the Curriculum: Methods of Integrating HIV/AIDS in Theological Programmes*, Geneva: WCC Publications, p. ix.

and indifference, and a lack of response by both faith communities and their training institutions. It became even more
evident in the explanation of the origin of the epidemic. The
disease was associated with punishment for sin and immorality of those who are suffering. This perspective contributed
towards creating a second epidemic, namely, stigma and discrimination of those with HIV/AIDS, intensifying the suffering of the infected and affected through social isolation,
rejection, fear and hopelessness. Before we knew it, the
stigma of HIV/AIDS had carried the epidemic to greater
depth – from just a physical disease that had infected some
parts of nations to a social epidemic that affected us all.[9]

In the extract forming Chapter 6, Dube takes account of the
Synoptic Jesus' prophetic role in siding with the least privileged
members of his society and challenging faith practices tolerant
of social injustice. Jesus, she argues: took sides with the
marginalized members of the society such as tax collectors,
widows, sex workers, children and lepers; healed all forms of
sickness, without asking how the person got the illness; not only
healed lepers, who were feared and isolated, but also touched
them and restored them back to society; empowered women
and children; forgave sins for what was held to be immoral
lifestyles; questioned oppressive scriptures; and openly contested oppressive leaders. All of this, she believes, is directly
relevant to teaching about and fighting AIDS today.

There are obvious points of contact here with my own previously unpublished Chapter 7. I seek to explore the connection
that both Musa Dube and the Windhoek Report (as well as
many, many others) make between the way the Synoptic Jesus
responded to leprosy and the way in which we should respond
today to the challenge of AIDS. The comparison is made complicated and theologically interesting once it is realized that
none of the biblical references to 'leprosy' includes 'any of the
indubitable signs and symptoms of leprosy, and those that are
mentioned tell against rather than for leprosy'.[10] Indeed both

---

9 Dube, *HIV/AIDS and the Curriculum*, p. viii.
10 S. G. Browne, 1970, *Leprosy in the Bible*, London: Christian Medical
Fellowship, p. 8.

'leprosy' in the Bible and 'AIDS' in the modern world attract stigmatizing social perceptions that have little to do with epidemiology. Once this is realized I try to show what is distinctive and challenging about the Synoptic Jesus' response to 'lepers' and just how relevant this is to the challenge of AIDS today.

That, however, is not the end of the story. In my recent book *Health Care and Christian Ethics* (CUP, 2006) I argue that in several areas involving ethical responses to AIDS in the modern world there is a critical tension between the common good and the compassionate care of individuals. So, whereas an approach based upon the latter (the dominant approach in most of the chapters in the present book) is clearly required by Christian ethics responding to people living with HIV, it may still be in tension with public health attempts to control the spread of this dangerous virus. Or, to put this somewhat simplistically, there is an obvious tension between not stigmatizing individuals living with HIV while still stigmatizing forms of behaviour that endanger others. This tension is certainly present in the Windhoek Report since it states both that: 'If we have HIV or AIDS, we should expect that our churches treat us compassionately and without stigma'; *and* 'We have a responsibility to be faithful in our sexual relationships . . . a wilful lack of responsibility . . . is dangerous to other people and, on that account, sinful.' Of course the Report acknowledges that sexual relationships are not the only means of transmitting HIV infection and that using, say, dirty needles is also irresponsible, dangerous and therefore sinful. But even here it admits that 'HIV transmission occurs, in the vast majority of cases, as a result of sexual activity'. Condemning dangerous sexual activity while not condemning those who engage in it presents an obvious problem – a problem that Ryan and Moore both wrestle with in their chapters.

An adequate theological response should not ignore this tension. More than that, this is a tension that can be found already in the wisdom present in the Synoptic healing stories. In my recent book I argue:

The Synoptic Jesus shows anger towards the leper in Mark (1.43), anger towards the Pharisees in the story of the man with the withered hand (3.5), and in Matthew the two blind men are told 'sternly' by Jesus to tell no-one (9.30). In other words, Jesus is depicted as both caring for the ill and disabled and caring about the prevalence of illness and disability. The passionate emotions depicted in the Synoptic healing stories appear sometimes to be directed at the disease itself or at the 'unclean spirits' and at other times at the faithlessness of the disciples or the religious authorities of the time. Compassionate care for the vulnerable goes hand in hand with passionate care about the conditions that make them vulnerable.[11]

Denise Ackermann's 'AIDS and Theological Education' was originally published in February 2005 as part of UNAIDS, *A Report of a Theological Workshop Focusing on HIV- and AIDS-related Stigma*. Ackermann is an Anglican theologian, a native South African and Professor of Theology at the University of Stellenbosch. Her focus is very specifically upon theological education that takes the challenge of AIDS seriously. She suggests three ways of doing this: through the critical role of narrative in disseminating knowledge; through theological methodology that is alive to the creative tension between theory and praxis; and through critical analysis that is sensitive to issues of power. Like other contributors she addresses the subject of sexuality, 'emphasizing the call to mutual, caring relationships and the fact that human sexuality is a gift from God'. She also calls attention to the theologically distinctive role of 'lamentation' that is present in the Windhoek Report: 'Lament is risky and dangerous speech; it is restless; it pushes the boundaries of our relationships, particularly with God; it refuses to settle for things the way they are.' It differs sharply from the silence and lack of truth-telling that nourishes stigma. And she asks the sharp question: 'Why not teach our students about the richness of the tradition of lament as a means of countering the pain of HIV- and AIDS-related stigma?'

Chapter 9 was originally written for the Summer Mission Briefing of the conservative evangelical Oxford Centre for

---

11 Robin Gill, 2006, *Health Care and Christian Ethics*, Cambridge: Cambridge University Press, p. 151.

Mission Studies and contains an interesting mixture of conservative theology and more liberal pastoral practice. The extract here was first published in June 2005 as Stan Nussbaum (ed.), *The Contribution of Christian Congregations to the Battle with HIV/AIDS at the Community Level* (pp. 5–6, 34–6, 37, 39–42, 44–5 and 51–2). The report as a whole gathers together local church information from Zambia, Zimbabwe, Kenya, Nigeria, Honduras, India and Peru in order to examine 'what local Christian congregations are already doing to meet HIV/ AIDS needs in their communities and how their contribution could be increased'.[12] The editor Stan Nussbaum (Global Mapping International, Colorado Springs) emphasizes in the extract published here that 'the local congregational contribution to the HIV/AIDS battle' is both important and often unrecognized by governments and secular groups. Like other theologians represented in this book – Catholic and non-Catholic alike – Nussbaum believes that there are compelling theological reasons for Christians to respond actively to the challenge of AIDS. For him this is based upon a larger theological picture: 'a dynamic understanding of the core message of Christianity, a bias for the poor and suffering, and . . . a positive yet disciplined theology of sexuality'. A distinctive part of the extract is the extended argument that (evangelical) congregations need to make connections with secular agencies in responding to the challenge of AIDS and that there are important areas of overlap between the two. Table 9.1 sets out in summary form what Nussbaum believes are the 'shared Christian and secular agenda' and what are 'uniquely Christian agenda'. Negatively, he argues bluntly that: 'Many Christians assumed that preaching and moralizing about HIV/AIDS by church authorities would solve the problem. Many secular groups assumed that better information about HIV/AIDS would do the job. Millions are now dying of AIDS because of these theories, and the theories are dying a slow death with them.' Positively, he argues that local congregations can motivate

---

12 Stan Nussbaum (ed.), *The Contribution of Christian Congregations to the Battle with HIV/AIDS at the Community Level*, Global Mapping International: http://www.gmi.org/research/aids.htm, p. 2.

people better than secular agencies to act altruistically and to behave responsibly.

Margaret A. Farley has voiced an important feminist theological response to the challenge of AIDS.[13] She holds the Gilbert L. Stark Chair of Christian Ethics at Yale University Divinity School. In her 2002 'Madeleva Lecture in Spirituality' she champions a concept of 'compassionate respect' that seeks to do justice to the demands of both compassion and care. She takes an extended example of responses to AIDS, arguing that 'compassion', although crucial for those living with HIV infection or AIDS disease, is nonetheless inadequate on its own to prevent the spread of this global pandemic. She argues that 'compassion requires at its core not only love but truth – not only the passion of compassion but the truth that compels respect'.[14] As a Catholic feminist she is especially concerned about women in a context of AIDS:

> Why do women bear a disproportionate share in the burdens of the AIDS pandemic? Without power over their sexual lives, they have little control over occasions of infection. Whether they are pressured into marriages not of their choosing, or as widows coerced into sexual relations with relatives of former husbands, or prevented from the knowledge and medical assistance necessary to limit their childbearing, they live in a context where their subordination to men determines their health or sickness, life or death. Even in university settings, where education regarding sex and sexually-transmitted disease is presumably available, massive numbers of women students become infected.[15]

---

13 See also Pamela Couture and Bonnie Miller McLemore (eds), 2003, *Poverty, Suffering and HIV–AIDS: International Practical Theological Perspectives*, Cardiff: Cardiff Academic Press; and Maria Cimperman OSU, 2005, *When God's People Have HIV/AIDS: An Approach to Ethics*, Maryknoll, NY: Orbis.

14 Margaret A. Farley, 2002, *Compassionate Respect: A Feminist Approach to Medical Ethics and Other Questions*, New York/Mahwah, NJ: Paulist Press, p. 20.

15 Farley, *Compassionate Respect*, pp. 14–15.

In Chapter 10, extracted from her article 'Partnership in Hope: Gender, Faith, and Responses to HIV/AIDS in Africa', first published in the *Journal of Feminist Studies in Religion* (20, Spring, 2004, pp. 33–148), Farley develops these concerns further by outlining the Yale Divinity School Women's Initiative on AIDS. Following the White House World AIDS Day Summit in 2000, in which she took part, the United States Agency for International Development started a new programme focused on women in community-based organizations (including faith-based organizations) in the Southern Hemisphere. As part of this programme the Agency helped to establish the Women's Initiative at Yale Divinity School. The chapter outlines the work of this initiative that has as its central aim 'the mutual self-empowerment of women of faith, breaking the silence among themselves, identifying their own ways to respond to the AIDS pandemic'.

Chapter 11 depicts theological activism in a second area, namely counselling people living with AIDS. Gunther H. Wittenberg, Emeritus Professor of Old Testament Studies, School of Theology, University of Natal, published 'Counselling AIDS Patients: Job as a Paradigm' in the *Journal of Theology for Southern Africa* (88, 1994, pp. 61–8: an earlier version appeared in *Positive Outlook*, Spring 1993, pp. 14–15). In this innovative article Wittenberg is concerned less with the technique of counselling people living with AIDS than with the way in which different ways of interpreting the Bible (i.e. hermeneutics) can affect Christian counselling of those living with AIDS. He is conscious that 'religious language does not only liberate and lead to new perspectives and change, but it can also increase the agony of the patient' and he demonstrates at length how this can be so, using the book of Job. Viewed properly 'Job rejects a theology which starts with abstract theological concepts but ignores the concrete life situation, suffering and hope of human beings. What Job's friends are saying is predictable. They utter abstract theological "truths" which have no link with real life because they have never experienced Job's pain.' For Wittenberg such an understanding of Job is directly relevant to the counselling of AIDS patients (especially, of course, in South Africa where Christian churches remain strong). He insists that in the context of AIDS it is important to recognize: the ambivalence of religious language; the importance of using the language of protest and lament (as Ackermann also concludes in Chapter 8); and rediscovering real comfort in suffering through an encounter with God.

And Chapter 12 depicts theological activism in a third area, this time through a campaign to enable antiretroviral drugs to become available and affordable in South Africa. Lisa Sowle Cahill is J. Donald Monan, SJ, Professor of Theology at Boston College. A leading Roman Catholic feminist theologian, she is the author of *Sex, Gender and Christian Ethics* (Cambridge: Cambridge University Press, 1996) and *Family: A Christian Social Perspective* (Minneapolis: Fortress Press, 2000). This chapter is extracted from her article 'Bioethics, Theology and Social Change', *Journal of Religious Ethics* (31:3, 2003, pp. 365–71, 378–9, 381 and 385–6). She notes that many Christian ethicists lament their exclusion from public bioethics and the dominance of secular bioethical principles; 'religion became intimidated from "speaking in its own voice," or came to be viewed as able to speak with integrity only within "the confines of particular religious communities"'. She believes that: 'To a remarkable degree, the critics of "the Enlightenment Project" of secular discourse have bought into the terms of that project when they agree that influential public discourse not only is secular but is controlled by intellectual and scientific elites who are privileged arbiters of the direction government will take.' One result of this, she believes, is 'the never-ending advocacy of many churches, religious groups, and theologians for "pro-life causes"'. However, what such a theological approach over-looks is the significant role of churches as social activists at a more local level. And the particular example she gives of such local church activism is the 'series of events that in about a two-year period loosened the grip of major pharmaceutical companies on patented AIDS drugs, making them available cheaply or for free in countries with high rates both of poverty and of AIDS deaths, beginning with South Africa'. In her article 'Biotech Justice: Catching up with the Real World Order', also published in 2003 (*Hastings Center Report* 33:4, pp. 39–42), she gives a very detailed account of this ultimately successful campaign mounted by a variety of organizations, including churches in South Africa.

The final two chapters have been chosen to demonstrate at depth some of the ongoing theological debates especially among Catholic theologians. Precisely because traditional Catholic (and Evangelical Protestant) teaching on contraception appears often to clash with barrier methods of limiting HIV infection, there has been an important, and at times complex, theological debate among Catholic theologians responding to the challenge of AIDS. Catholics and Evangelical Protestants engaged in the pastoral care of people living with HIV infection frequently express conflicting views on the use of barrier methods of limiting HIV infection (as previous chapters have demonstrated). Both Leonard Martin and James Keenan, exploring respectively the Catholic theological concepts of the lesser good and a casuistry of accommodation, respond directly to this internal debate.

The Redemptorist moral theologian Leonard M. Martin participated in the Windhoek workshop shortly before his death. Originally from Ireland, he had lived and worked in Brazil for many years and was at the time of his death Titular Professor of Ethics at the State University of Ceará, Fortaleza, Brazil. In a previously unpublished essay (written for a conference in San Salvador in September 2001), forming Chapter 13 here, he argued that rigorist Catholic teaching alone will not prevent the spread of AIDS. In pastoral terms it may actually be counter-productive, with many ordinary people drawing 'the conclusion that religious people in general and Catholic moral theology in particular has nothing more to say to them'. As a result they may 'follow the line that since total sexual abstinence before marriage is not possible, and since it and only it is deemed acceptable, then there is no point in any type of restraint'. This observation prompted Martin to explore the concept of 'the lesser evil'. Following Brian Johnstone he explored the argument that 'a counsellor may propose to a person infected with the HIV virus, who will not abstain from sexual activity, that he or she use a condom rather than risk transmitting the lethal virus, causing the death of the partner, and transforming himself into a culpable killer'. From a traditional Catholic perspective such a use of a condom might then be considered to be a 'lesser evil'. However, Martin was not altogether happy with this 'ecclesiastical solution' since 'from the point of view of those who do not share that world-view, it can be patronising and offensive'. Instead, Martin argued for a pastoral response in terms of a concept of 'lesser good' that shows 'respect for the integrity of people's consciences and for what they perceive to be good'.

The Jesuit theologian James F. Keenan suggests, instead, a broader pastoral approach based upon the Catholic concept of the 'casuistry of accommodation'. He is Professor of Moral Theology at the Weston Jesuit School of Theology in Cambridge, Massachusetts, and is editor of *Catholic Ethicists of HIV/AIDS Prevention* (New York/London: Continuum, 2000) and, with Thomas Shannon, *The Context of Casuistry* (Washington: Georgetown University, 1995). He has done more than most other academic theologians to generate an appropriate and compassionate theological response to the challenge of AIDS. Chapter 14 is extracted from the longer article 'Applying the Seventeenth-Century Casuistry of Accommodation to HIV Prevention' that he wrote in 1999 for the journal *Theological Studies* (60:3, pp. 492–3 and 500–12). In the first half of the original article (which is too long to reproduce here) Keenan traces the way that casuistry – or the study of cases – has functioned in the Catholic Church over the last 500 years (a point also noted by Cahill). Following Albert Jonsen and Stephen Toulmin's *The Abuse of Casuistry* (Berkeley: University of California, 1988) he locates the beginning of high casuistry in the mid-sixteenth century and the development of a 'casuistry of accommodation' in the seventeenth century:

Casuistry in the 16th century was evidently very different from casuistry in the 17th century. The former was about cases breaking open the claims of a principle and eventually replacing the principle. It was a casuistry of its age, the age of discovery. In this casuistry, cases and not principles served as analogous guides for a very inductive form of logic. In the 17th century, however, with the articulation of new material principles, casuistry was rather deductive; there was no interest in prolonging the upheaval of the 16th century . . . The 17th century developed those methodological principles [such as double effect, lesser evil, cooperation in wrongdoing, totality, and toleration] that allowed moralists to consider chaotic issues that were not covered by the material principle.[16]

Keenan gives a twentieth-century example of the latter, namely Pope Pius XII sanctioning the application of dangerous dosages of morphine in the cases of people inevitably dying in terrible pain. Using the doctrine of double effect it was considered possible for Catholic leaders to sanction this new medical application for such cases without undermining their material principle against euthanasia. Such use of a 'casuistry of accommodation', Keenan argues in this final chapter, has made it possible that: 'for the past four centuries Catholic moral logic has been faithful to its clear principles and at the same time has been consistently willing to consider new cases, which it resolved without compromising the existing material principles. It did this by a fairly broad selection of methodological principles that allowed casuists to recognize new claims that were not covered by the material principles.'

There is, of course, an ongoing debate among Catholic theologians, among non-Catholic theologians and between Catholic and non-Catholic theologians about the applicability and veracity of methodological principles such as double effect, lesser evil and so forth. This is to be expected and it is no purpose of this book to resolve this debate. However, what Keenan's contribution admirably shows is that there is a serious level of sophistication and compassion evident in at least some theological responses to the challenge of AIDS. Seven years after Keenan made the predictions in this chapter there are also interesting signs (as other chapters have indicated) that they may be coming true:

We have every reason to believe that in time, more bishops will not directly censure health care workers in Catholic

---

16 *Theological Studies* 60:3, p. 498.

facilities who in conscience recommend to their clients that they protect the common good, by abstinence, and failing that, by prophylactic measures. Likewise, we should not expect the censure of moral theologians who assert the liceity of spouses protecting one another from their infection. And we can reasonably expect to see Catholic hospitals becoming progressively involved in needle exchange.

Keenan ends his chapter with a call for compassion. He argues that 'the tradition gave us the casuistry of accommodation, precisely because the tradition is animated at its best moments by the virtue of mercy'. That, I believe, is a fitting note on which to conclude this Introduction. Following the Synoptic Jesus, compassion surely should be our primary response to the challenge and tragedy of so many of our fellow human beings living with untreated HIV infection and AIDS disease today.

1. The Windhoek Report: HIV- and AIDS-related stigma – A framework for theological reflection

Report from UNAIDS International Workshop for Academic Theologians from different Christian traditions, held at Windhoek, Namibia 8–11 December 2003.

Introduction

In the context of HIV and AIDS, the most powerful obstacle to effective prevention, treatment and care is proving to be the stigmatization of people living with HIV and AIDS. Christian theology has, sometimes unintentionally, operated in such a way as to reinforce the stigma, and to increase the likelihood of discrimination. However, at other times, Christian theology has also, often, been successful in challenging society's injustices and bringing about change. Examples include the theological bases on which reformers argued for the abolition of slavery, and also the theological process that led to the Kairos document, which played such a notable part in hastening the end of structural apartheid in South Africa.

Stigma is difficult to define. Generally, though, it implies the branding or labelling of a person or a group of persons as being unworthy of inclusion in human community, and it results in discrimination and ostracization. The branding or labelling is usually related to some perceived physical, psychological or moral condition believed to render the individual unworthy of full inclusion in the community. We may stigmatize those we regard as impure, unclean or dangerous, those who are different from ourselves or live in different ways, or those who are simply strangers. In the process we construct damaging stereotypes and perpetuate injustice and discrimination. Stigma often involves a conscious or unconscious exercise of power over the vulnerable and marginalized.

The purpose of the present document is to identify those aspects of Christian theology that endorse or foster stigmatizing attitudes and behaviour towards people living with HIV and AIDS and those around them, and to suggest what resources exist within Christian theology that might enable churches to develop more positive and loving approaches. It is not a theological statement, but rather a framework for theological thinking, and an opportunity, for church leaders, to pursue a deeper Christian reflection on the current crisis.

We have identified the following major theological themes as ones that need to be addressed in any structured reflection on HIV- and AIDS-related stigma:

- God and Creation
- interpreting the Bible
- sin
- suffering and lamentation
- covenantal justice
- truth and truth-telling; and
- the Church as a healing, inclusive and accompanying community.

God and Creation

At the heart of the stigmatizing attitudes to HIV and AIDS that can be found within the churches lie widely differing understandings of God. Sometimes Christians have presented a model of a vindictive God who inflicts HIV and AIDS as a punishment for human sin. In contrast, we believe that God is a God of compassion, who delights in creation. HIV is a virus (extremely dangerous to human beings), but not a divine punishment for sin.

God created us as unique persons and differentiated beings. God delights in our differences, and invites us to do the same. God created us as sexual human beings in all our differences.

This is to be celebrated, enjoyed and treated responsibly. The story of the Garden of Eden is partly the story of human beings' alienation from their sexuality. God's gift to us is the capacity to enjoy one another as sexual beings, and it is we who have squandered that gift. God created us for one another and for God, and wants us to celebrate the gift of sexuality through which God's Creation unfolds.

The embodied human being is the temple of the Lord. The abuse of bodies is therefore an offence, both against God and against God's Creation, as well as being a sinful exercise of power. This includes the abuse, by men, of the bodies of women. Men and women are created equally. In honouring one another as sexual beings, we are honouring life itself. And yet HIV transmission is often linked with the vulnerability and abuse of women or of young boys or girls. Women cannot protect themselves from HIV, nor can children, if their sexuality is controlled by others.

Images of God have often been used to support patriarchy, while interpretations of the book of Genesis have led to the stigmatization of women's sexuality. These misreadings of the scriptures have hampered the Church's attempts to engage with the stigmatization of people living with HIV and AIDS and have thus diminished its capacity to help prevent HIV transmission.

God is present with the vulnerable and, in a special way, with stigmatized people.

We need to reclaim (and also to communicate to Christian believers) biblical images of God that are Trinitarian, non-patriarchal and grounded not in punishment but in divine love.

Interpreting the Bible

Christian faith, as shown in the Bible, is central to Christianity. The Bible tells the story of God's ongoing concern for Creation and humanity, and in doing so it has much to teach us about stigma. Nevertheless, the Bible has often been read and interpreted in such a way as to encourage stigmatizing attitudes and practices within the Church, and to increase the stigmatization of the vulnerable and marginalized.

Historically the churches have often used the Bible for purposes of exclusion. In the context of stigmatization, attempts are being made to discover and reclaim texts that foster inclusion. It is not possible to find, in the Bible, an exact parallel to the stigmatization of those living with HIV and AIDS: and yet within biblical tradition there are many examples that point to the way in which the stigmatized of the day were treated. We need to learn from the manner in which Jesus related to and responded to the stigmatized, for example lepers, Samaritans, a menstruating woman, and those with physical and emotional disabilities. Jesus mixed with them, included them, invited them into his circle of friends, touched them and, in turn, allowed himself to be touched by them. In the end Jesus submitted himself to the ultimate stigmatization of public crucifixion outside the city walls.

In seeking to reclaim these destigmatizing readings of the Bible, the following points may be made.

- The scriptures themselves were written in particular contexts, at different times, and they reflect the social locations of the authors.
- When we choose texts to support stigma, we are often refusing to acknowledge our own social context and the cultural traditions that have shaped our views.
- The two consistent themes of scripture are God's love and God's justice, by which God seeks to redeem Creation and humanity.
- Since God's abiding concern is for our well-being or fullness of life, no passage from scripture should be used to diminish this in any other human being.
- The life, death and resurrection of Jesus Christ offer hope and new life to all of humanity. They deal a death blow to all stigmas. They affirm the human worth shared by all humanity, created as we are in the divine image and sanctified by Christ's sacrifice.

Readings of the Bible must be Christ-centred and linked to the context in which we find ourselves. We need to acknowledge insights, now available to us, which were not available to the biblical authors and previous generations of people studying or reading the Bible. These include the findings of modern biblical scholarship, and relevant anthropological and sociological research on biblical themes. They also include insights gained from contextual theologies, and from a deepening understanding, within the Church, of issues of social justice.

Sin

Biblical faith understands sin relationally, namely as the breaking of our essential relatedness to God, to one another and to the rest of Creation. Sin, therefore, is alienation and estrangement, and infects us all. Whether we have HIV or not, we are all sinners. As communities and as individuals, we have fallen short of the glory of God. To stigmatize the other is to deny this truth.

Understandings of sin, therefore, constitute an essential component of HIV- and AIDS-related stigma. Within this relationship, four main strands can be identified.

The sin of stigmatizing

The stigmatization of individuals is a sin against the Creator God, in whose image all human beings are made. To stigmatize an individual is to reject the image of God in the other, and to deny him or her life in all its fullness. This is not just a sin against a neighbour but also a sin against God.

The association between sexuality and sin

The stigmatization of people living with HIV and AIDS has grown out of the mistaken link, often made in Christian thinking, between sexuality and sin. It includes the widely held assumption that HIV is always contracted as the result of 'sinful' sexual relations, and the additional tendency to regard sexual sin as the gravest of all sins. So sex may come to carry the stigma of sinfulness, and is also stigmatized among other sins. Consequently, people living with HIV and AIDS are subjected to a deeper stigmatization that sets them apart from the so-called 'lesser' sinners.

It is true that HIV transmission occurs, in the vast majority of cases, as a result of sexual activity. But far from being inherently sinful, the responsible use of sex and human sexuality is part of God's Creation, to be celebrated and enjoyed. Within the context of faith today, there is a need to denounce the identification of sin with sex, as well as the stigmatization and the debased theology of sin that results from it. (It should also be stressed that HIV transmission does not result solely from sexual activity, and that unhygienic methods of collecting blood, failure by governments to screen blood donations, and the use of shared needles for injecting drugs can also cause HIV transmission.)

HIV and AIDS as punishment for sin

It is wrong to interpret HIV and AIDS (or other human catastrophes) as God's punishment for sin. This interpretation is damaging, because the judgemental attitudes that result are highly undermining to the Church's efforts at care and prevention. It is also theologically unsustainable, a fact that is demonstrated powerfully in the book of Job, and also in many of the healing narratives of the Gospels. In reflecting on the connections between HIV transmission and sin, it is important to remember that many people who become infected bear no responsibility for their condition: namely babies born with the virus, abused women and children, and faithful partners of unfaithful spouses.

Sin as failure to take responsibility

The threat posed by the HIV pandemic requires that human beings should act responsibly. We have a responsibility to be faithful in our sexual relationships. Those with HIV or AIDS have a special responsibility not to risk infecting other people. Those who screen donated blood have a responsibility to be vigilant. And those taking blood or injecting drugs have a responsibility to ensure that the needles are sterile. A wilful lack of responsibility in any of these areas is dangerous to other people, and, on that account, sinful.

In summary, if we are to combat stigma effectively, we need a more positive Christian understanding of sexuality focused upon faithfulness, kindness and the care and protection of families. If we have HIV or AIDS, we should expect that our churches treat us compassionately and without stigma. The stigmatization of others is a sin far greater than most of the so-called 'misdeeds' on which HIV infection is often blamed. After all, the sinful attitudes, most frequently identified by Jesus as being incompatible with his Kingdom, were pride, self-righteousness, exclusivity, hypocrisy and the misuse of power: all of them ingredients in the deadly cocktail that causes stigma.

Suffering and lamentation

As embodied and relational people we suffer. However, suffering has sometimes been considered a given, the unavoidable destiny of individuals. On other occasions, it has been regarded as a punishment for sin. Suffering may also be inappropriately exalted as a virtue. These interpretations have no place in Christian theology, which needs, rather, to emphasize the redemptive aspect of suffering, and to challenge those social structures that cause undue suffering and stigma. Jesus, after all, showed compassion for the suffering: a compassion that involved both strong feeling for suffering individuals and a determination to help and empower them. In the cross of Jesus, God enters the suffering Creation to heal it from within. Jesus showed solidarity with us, and compassion. On the cross Jesus died, stigmatized and outcast, outside the city walls.

In gaining better insights into the nature of suffering and our response to it, we can seek to recover biblical texts on suffering, and in this context it is helpful to draw on the rich biblical tradition of lament. Lament primarily articulates the cries of the suffering, but it can also give voice to the cries of the guilty seeking forgiveness and reconciliation. Lament offers us language which names the suffering, questions power structures, calls for justice and recounts to God that the human situation should be otherwise. Lament also expresses hope and trust in God's compassion and willingness to deliver us from suffering. It is both an individual and a communal activity. Given circumstances which (in St John Chrysostom's words) are 'grazed thin by death', how can we fail to lament? Thus lament can enrich church liturgies and pastoral care and contribute to a more truthful and intimate relationship with God by naming the 'un-nameable' to God.

Covenantal justice

The biblical concept of covenant implies a reciprocal, binding relationship between God and human beings, which should be mirrored in the relationships that human beings have with one another. Just as God has given us the grace to ask for God's friendship, human beings can justly ask certain things of the societies they build. However, the needs of the powerless are easily overlooked, especially if they are carrying the double stigma of poverty and HIV or AIDS.

It is no coincidence that HIV and AIDS are raging in the developing world. Of course impoverishment does not, of itself, cause HIV infection: the virus has manifestly affected both rich and poor in different parts of the world. Nevertheless it does exacerbate the problem. It leaves people economically poor, hungry, illiterate and with inadequate access to health-care services. In this situation, the impact of HIV and AIDS stretches poor nations' already limited resources to breaking point and makes it less likely that prevention strategies and caring programmes will succeed.

It is not enough to tackle the symptoms of poverty, although there are moments when such intervention is appropriate. In the long term, we must identify the root causes of impoverishment, which often lie in deliberately chosen political, social and economic policies. Unfortunately, rulers at local and national levels are often relatively powerless when it comes to taking on the banks and multinational corporations with whom many of the strategic economic and political decisions lie. Nevertheless, political leadership should be challenged about the misuse of public resources, and this includes the disproportionate use of national budgets to acquire armaments, rather than allocating them to health, education and basic services for the poor. In a world disfigured by AIDS, we need especially to address political corruption.

Churches have tended to engage with the symptoms and condemn the causes, while failing to explore ways of addressing poverty's structural roots. For example, we are sometimes compromised because of our dependence, for support of our ministry, on those who make their wealth in poor nations. As theologians, we have not sufficiently promoted the Church's social teaching, or challenged the Church to rediscover its prophetic voice and ministry.

While some churches in the global North have responded to the needs of their sisters and brothers in Christ in the South, there still exists a lack of global solidarity among those who claim unity in the Body of Christ. If we truly believe that HIV and AIDS are in the Church, then no part of the Body of Christ is left unaffected, regardless of the separations imposed by geography, culture or tradition. The theological challenge to the churches must therefore be to re-examine their priorities in terms of ministry and of budgets, as they seek to engage with this crisis, this *kairos* moment.

Truth and truth-telling

Stigma feeds on silence and denial. Individuals sometimes keep quiet about their fears of being HIV-positive because they are too afraid to seek help for themselves or their families. Institutions and communities may fear the stigma that will fall on them if members are found to be carrying a stigmatized condition. Thus the dread of stigmatization becomes more powerful than the demands of truth or the longing for wholeness.

This raises a number of theological challenges, for churches as well as for individuals. What should they teach or not teach about HIV, particularly to young people? What should they say or not say about individual members? What should individuals disclose or keep secret about themselves? How can our communities move beyond denial and become more accepting of those who speak the truth?

Jesus taught us that truth sets us free, and gave us the mandate to teach truth. However, churches often find this difficult. The truth sometimes exposes the gap between what their leaders and members preach and what they actually do. This creates a huge problem for individuals, for whom the disclosure of stigmatizing information in an unsympathetic, stigmatizing environment can be a fearsome and risky under-taking.

In relation to HIV and AIDS, experience has shown that the best form of prevention is truthful education. This applies to 'truths of fact' (what HIV is, how it is transmitted, how it can be prevented, and what will happen if a person becomes infected); but it also applies to 'truth of meaning', which is a theme which churches are well fitted to explore. 'Truth of meaning' relates to the meaning of suffering, the nature of sin, the relationship between life and death, and the search for the mind of God.

There is an urgent need to build communities that are wel-coming, supportive and capable of breaking the silence about HIV and AIDS. Many churches are committed, in principle, to doing this. But it is hard to see how they can succeed without some painful soul-searching at the level of the institutions them-selves, as well as of their hierarchies, clergy and members. For churches, truth-telling may involve an acknowledgement that they have been party to stigmatization. They may have advo-cated 'bad theology' or failed to challenge it. They may have condoned a climate of silence and denial at institutional level, diluted or misrepresented the facts in their educational pro-grammes, failed to provide strong, prophetic leadership, and been responsible for the poor moral example which sometimes exists within the churches themselves. It must be remembered that Jesus was particularly critical of religious people when he caught them out in hypocrisy.

The Church as a healing, inclusive and accompanying community

The stigmatization of people living with HIV and AIDS calls the Church to ask itself what it means, in our time, to be the inclusive community that Jesus proclaimed. Churches have a fine record in the care of people living with HIV and AIDS and their families, care of orphans, and support for the families of those who have died; while today, in the context of HIV and AIDS, some churches are stretched to breaking point by the burden of funerals and of ministry to the sick and dying. But these efforts have not always been successful in tackling the stigma attached to HIV and AIDS.

As a community of disciples of Jesus Christ, the Church should be a sanctuary, a safe place, a refuge, a shelter for the stigmatized and the excluded. The Church is called to work towards both the prevention of stigma and the care of the stigmatized. And yet churches have habitually excluded and stigmatized those who were 'different', those who did not conform, and those who have sinned or were thought to have sinned. This challenges our understanding of the Church's identity, and calls for deeper reflection on the issue of inclusion and exclusion within our communities. Jesus' ministry was inclusive to the point of scandalizing religious authorities and so-called 'respectable' people. In a time when people living with HIV and AIDS are being stigmatized and discriminated against within our churches, this suggests the need for renewed theological reflection on the nature and identity of the Church itself.

If we acknowledge suffering we must be prepared to respond, and many church leaders are realizing the need for help and support at parish level. However, sometimes our ability to accompany suffering people is restricted by our lack of confidence, and by our sense that we do not have the necessary resources. Education is therefore needed for churches trying to accompany those who are carrying the stigma of HIV or AIDS. Also required is much sensitivity to the fears the stigmatized person may have about disclosure or further rejection. Appropriate resources will enable clergy, laity, and in particular young people to respond, so that the Church may fulfil its task in a responsible, loving and dialogical way.

This role needs to be explored at the level of theological education, so that clergy and lay leaders go into parishes with some understanding of the dynamics of accompanying stigmatized and suffering people, of praying with them and their families, of 'standing and waiting' alongside them, and of loving them into hope.

In addressing stigma, people living with HIV and AIDS are the churches' most precious resource. They have been described as the 'wounded healers' of our time. Their full inclusion in all aspects of the Church's life is the best possible strategy for changing attitudes and removing fear. The experience of living with HIV or AIDS raises profound questions about the meaning of suffering and the nature of God; and in sharing these insights, the spirituality of the whole worshipping community may be enriched. People living with HIV or AIDS have commented that the liturgies and rituals of the Church have been a great source of strength, particularly when they are combined with the support of the worshipping community.

In our reflections on a Church that says 'No' to stigma, we need constantly to revisit the Christ of the Gospel narratives, who has given us a paradigm for accompaniment, human relationships and Christian healing. We believe that our scriptures encourage us to move beyond the stigmatization and exclusion of the crucifixion towards resurrection, hope and redemption. The Church must remain a Church of hope even in a context of HIV and AIDS.

2. The Human and Pastoral Challenges of HIV and AIDS

ROBERT J. VITILLO

It might be argued that the most urgent ethical issue arising from the pandemic of HIV and AIDS is the lack of distributive justice. The poorest, most marginalized and oppressed members of society are also most vulnerable to the threat of HIV and the tragic consequences of AIDS. They are deprived of access to the preventive education, care, treatment and support which they urgently need.

Such inequitable access is intimately linked to the personal and family well-being, or lack thereof, among those affected by the pandemic. Availability of combination, antiretroviral therapy is a particular case in point. In the United States, public and private spending on HIV and AIDS averages at US$30,000 per person, per year. However, in low- and middle-income countries AIDS funding still is relatively minuscule. For example, Kenya spends US$0.76 *per capita* on AIDS, and US$12.92 *per capita* on debt repayments. One can easily identify a cause–effect relationship between the 3 million deaths due to AIDS last year and the lack of availability of antiretroviral medications among those living with AIDS in low- and middle-income countries. It was based on such a conclusion that the World Heath Organization developed its '3 by 5 Initiative' to work toward the provision of antiretroviral medications to 3 million people in developing countries by 2005.

Global spending was just under US$5 billion in 2003. By the year 2007, however, approximately US$20 billion will be needed to meet a range of needs: to provide antiretroviral therapy to just over 6 million people; support 22 million orphans; provide HIV counselling and testing to 100 million adults; provide school-based HIV/AIDS education to 900 million students; and offer peer counselling services to 60 million out-of-school young people.[1] In case some of you question how the global community can generate the funds to provide such medications and services to so many people, let us not forget that an estimated $52 billion per year is spent in the United States in order to cope with the medical consequences of obesity.[2]

In his statement to the UN Special Session on HIV and AIDS, Cardinal Javier Lozano Barragan clearly stated the position of the Holy See with regard to the economic imbalances that constitute both the causes and effects of vulnerability occurring in relation to the pandemic of HIV and AIDS:

> An important factor contributing to the rapid spread of AIDS is the situation of extreme poverty experienced by a great part of humanity. Certainly a decisive factor in combating the disease is the promotion of social justice, in order to bring about a situation in which economic consideration would no longer serve as the sole criterion in an uncontrolled globalisation.[3]

Until very recently, I felt quite satisfied with the response of the Church to issues related to distributive justice. National and diocesan Caritas agencies, located in more than 200 countries of the world, have responded valiantly to disasters and to the ongoing effects of poverty alike. Even in the specific area of outreach to people affected by HIV and AIDS, Catholic hospitals and church-based social service and development organizations, including our own Catholic Relief Services' Africa Rising Campaign and Catholic Medical Mission Board's Born to Live Initiative, were among the first and the most effective to provide

---

1 Yvette Collymore, July 2004, Population Reference Bureau.
2 UNAIDS, December 2000, *Report on the Global Situation of AIDS*.
3 Archbishop Javier Lozano Barragan, intervention of the Holy See delegation to the UN Special Session on AIDS, New York, June 2001.

in-patient and home-based care, to establish blood safety and prevention of HIV transmission from mother to child pro-grammes (especially in rural areas), and to arrange for the schooling and guidance of AIDS orphans who cannot be assisted in their extended families. In fact, the Vatican's Pontifical Council for Health Care estimates that 25% of all HIV and AIDS care throughout the world is sponsored by the Catholic Church.

The Church also has used its moral authority and public credibility to advocate for the transformation of structural injustices that make people poor and therefore vulnerable to HIV and AIDS and countless other current ills. At the United Nations and in other international fora, the Holy See and Catholic non-governmental organizations advocate for poverty reduction strategies, debt relief for the poorest countries, a more equitable distribution of the world's goods, and greater access for the poor to basic medicines as well as the combina-tion antiretroviral therapies. Similarly, individual Catholics are encouraged to raise their political voices – when they are accorded such by their respective governments – to pressure national and local leaders toward a more just treatment of the poor and vulnerable: one that is worthy of the dignity accorded by God to all his children.

Despite all these excellent efforts, however, when I take into account the immensity of the impact wrought by this pandemic, especially on the poorest of the poor, I regrettably must conclude that the members and institutions of the Church have far more to do. In addition to the millions of dollars we have invested in church-sponsored education, health and social services, billions more are needed. We must dedicate more of the Church's economic and human resources to eliminating poverty as well as the tragic consequences of HIV and AIDS. Individual Christians and church institutions must, in the words of Pope John Paul II, give not just of their 'surplus' but also of their 'substance'.[4] Thus Cardinal Renato Martino, Head of the Holy See delegation to the United Nations International

---

4 Pope John Paul II, address at Yankee Stadium during visit to USA, 1979.

Conference on Financing Development, declared: 'the Family of Nations cannot allow one more day to pass wherein a real attempt to meet goals and make measurable progress toward the eradication of poverty is not pursued with all of the energy and resolve that [it] can muster'.[5]

Power inequities

A second major ethical issue related to the HIV and AIDS crisis is rooted in the imbalance of power in social, economic and gender relations. One egregious manifestation of power in-equity can be found in the oppression that men are allowed to exert over women.

So we note the following tragic trends.

In addition to the particular biological vulnerability of women and girls to contracting HIV, they are confronted almost daily with their relative lack of control over personal health and sexual activity as well as over the sexual activity of their partners. They cannot negotiate, still less refuse, sexual relations within marriage. Yet these same women often are blamed as 'vectors of HIV', even when they have been utterly faithful to their husbands, and the entry of the virus into the family circle has come from their husbands' infidelity.

Poverty all too often forces women and children to enter into prostitution to support themselves and their families, and in some circumstances families will even sell their children into prostitution in order to pay off debts or to advance the family's financial security. Sexual violence in many societies can be a contributing factor to the spread of HIV. In Kenya, a nation-wide study of 12- to 24-year-old women found that one in four is forced into intercourse as a first sexual experience. In South Africa, an estimated 370,000 women are raped every year.[6]

---

5 Archbishop Renato R. Martino, 'Development is First and Foremost a Question of People', Holy See's delegation at the UN International Conference on Financing Development, Monterrey, Mexico, 24 March 2002, www.zenit.org.

6 Catholic Relief Services, 16 February 2001, *Interim Standards and Approaches for CRS HIV and AIDS Programs in Africa*, p. 5.

Sexual abuse has also arisen as a result of the HIV pandemic, or more specifically from efforts to avoid becoming HIV infected. In many parts of the world, men have decreased their reliance on prostitutes because of the widespread fear of contracting HIV. As a result, many have turned to young (and therefore presumably uninfected) girls for sexual favours. In addition, anecdotal reports indicate that, in some cultures, the popular belief that sex with a virgin can cure an HIV-infected man leads to the rape of women and children who are thought to be virgins. Sadly, some incidents of such abuse have taken place within church circles.

In an attempt to discourage gender inequity, the Southern African Catholic Bishops' Conference issued the following admonition to young men: 'Respect girls and young women and relate to them without making sexual demands of them. St Paul says, "God wills you all to be holy. He wants you to keep away from sexual immorality" (1 Thessalonians 4.3).'[7]

For centuries, the Church has extended its services to women in need, including those with HIV and AIDS. In his message to the 1995 United Nations Fourth World Conference on the Concerns of Women, held in Beijing, Pope John Paul II committed 'the 300,000 social, educational and caring institutions of the Catholic Church to give priority to women and young girls, especially the poorest'.[8] During his greeting to the General Assembly of the World Union of Catholic Women's Organizations, held in 2001, the Holy Father reaffirmed that commitment: 'Working together, you must seek to provide increasing material and moral support to women in difficulty, victims of poverty and violence.'[9] These words of the bishops and of the Holy Father, although quite inspiring, will require much more active commitment and practical resources from the Church in order to truly bear fruit. Moreover, any acts of violence against

---

7 South African Catholic Bishops' Conference, 30 July 2001, 'A Message of Hope to the People of God from the Catholic Bishops of South Africa, Botswana and Swaziland'.

8 Pope John Paul II, message to the co-ordinator of the World Conference on Women, Beijing, August 1995.

9 Pope John Paul II, greeting to General Assembly of World Council of Catholic Women's Organizations (WUCWO), 7 March 2001.

women that are committed by church representatives or employees simply cannot be tolerated. I steadfastly believe that any claims of sexual violence against women or children perpetrated by church workers – clergy, religious or laity – must be afforded immediate, diligent and unbiased investigation, careful determination and a firm commitment to remove the employee from the position of trust if the claim is found to be credible. If the Church wishes to exert the moral force of its foundation in scripture and tradition, then she must prove herself to be a model in respecting the dignity and integrity of women and children.

Stigmatization and marginalization

An almost instinctive reaction to HIV disease has been that of discrimination against and stigmatization of HIV-infected people. Attempts to 'cast out' those affected by the disease – from villages, hospitals, educational institutions and faith communities – have been experienced in virtually all parts of the world and among all racial and ethnic groups, as well as in all social and economic classes. Sadly, some priests and ministers have refused pastoral care and church burial to the HIV infected. Many governments at one time or another have enacted policies of forced isolation and restriction of travel by HIV-infected persons, while others have tolerated, and even encouraged, violence toward such individuals. This discriminatory behaviour tends to create fear and secretive activity, even among those who already have basic knowledge about the pandemic. Studies in Côte d'Ivoire and South Africa show that, in places with extremely high HIV prevalence, women refused HIV testing or did not return for their results. In southern Africa, a study on needle stick injuries in primary health-care clinics found that nurses did not report the injuries because they did not want to be tested for HIV. In one study on home-care schemes, fewer than one in ten people who were caring for an HIV-infected patient at home acknowledged that their relative was suffering from the effects of this virus.[10]

---

10 UNAIDS, *Report*.

Research carried out in India, Indonesia, the Philippines and Thailand has evidenced such prejudice by friends and employees, and in workplace and health-care settings. In similar research carried out in four Nigerian states, one in ten care providers refused to serve HIV-positive patients and 20% indicated their belief that many people living with HIV had behaved immorally and 'deserved' to be infected.

Pope John Paul II has made frequent and emotional appeals to avoid discriminatory treatment of people living with HIV and AIDS. In his visit to AIDS patients in the United States in 1989 he held out the unconditional love of God himself as the guideline to be followed:

> God loves you all, without distinction, without limit . . . He loves those of you who are sick, those suffering from AIDS. He loves the friends and relatives of the sick and those who care for them. He loves all with an unconditional and ever-lasting love.[11]

The bishops of the Southern Africa Catholic Bishops' Conference leave no room for any possibility of stigmatization or marginalization based on the false premise that God has 'willed' AIDS for sinful individuals:

> *AIDS must never be considered as a punishment from God.* He wants us to be healthy and not to die from AIDS. It is for us a sign of the times challenging all people to inner transformation and to the following of Christ in his ministry of healing, mercy and love.[12]

The bishops of Ghana were among the first Episcopal voices to be raised in appeal for an unconditional and accepting response among Christians to the brokenness in human relationships that both precedes and results from HIV infection:

> AIDS often involves alienation and separation between the person with the disease and every surrounding system. We

---

11 Pope John Paul II, address given at Mission Dolores, 1989.
12 'A Message of Hope'.

are challenged to be reconcilers, helping to restore a sense of wholeness to broken relationships between the patient and those near to him or her. We must build a sense of trust and caring. This requires, education , and a change of heart . . .

If the yardstick of our faith is unconditional love, particularly love of those whom society regards as outcasts, then our response to people suffering from AIDS will be a measure of our faith.[13]

Despite the fact that the rejection and scapegoating of people affected by HIV and AIDS finds no basis in theological scholarship, such incidents continue to occur. While visiting many different countries to facilitate HIV and AIDS workshops for pastoral personnel, I have heard the 'horror stories' of pastors refusing to anoint HIV-infected people or forcing them to publicly confess the 'sins' that caused them to be infected. I believe that members of the hierarchy, clergy and laity alike have the responsibility to stop such poor pastoral practices as soon as they occur. I received much personal inspiration from an archbishop in a Caribbean country who, upon hearing that his priests were unwilling to visit a woman of supposed 'ill repute' and suffering with AIDS-related illnesses, went to visit her in the hospital and continued to do so on a daily basis, until the woman died. Then he celebrated her funeral Mass in his cathedral.

Privacy, confidentiality and responsibility

Another ethical issue emerging from the pandemic centres on the right to confidentiality which should be enjoyed by all people with regard to information about intimate details of their lives and welfare. Because of ignorance and fear, many people, including some members of the clergy, believe that HIV can be spread by ordinary social contact or through the air, and thus that all HIV-infected people must be identified publicly in order to avoid infection.

---

13 Ghana Bishops' Conference, October 1990, *Pastoral Statement on AIDS*.

Instead of adopting and rigorously following 'universal pre-cautions' (health-care policies that protect against transmission of HIV and other blood-borne diseases from any patient), some medical personnel claim that extraordinary measures need to be taken with patients known, or suspected, to be HIV infected, and thus insist on mandatory HIV testing and labelling of patients. By disregarding the patient's right to confidentiality, such irrational fears and policies undermine the dignity and human rights of those concerned. The Church's perspective on matters related to confidentiality and privacy of information is so strongly held that it is referenced in Canon Law: 'No one may unlawfully harm the good reputation which a person enjoys, or violate the right of every person to privacy' (Canon 220). The Bishops of the United States also addressed this issue, especially with regard to church workers who are affected by HIV: 'Every precaution should be taken to protect the confidentiality of records, files and other information about the HIV status of employees.'[14]

I have no reason to doubt that the clergy take seriously their sacred obligation to maintain secrecy about information that is shared with them in the confessional. However, I am well aware that many professionals – doctors, nurses, social workers, priests outside the confessional and other pastoral agents – often engage in petty gossip about the moral character of people living with HIV and AIDS and pursue curious rumination about which behaviours led to the infection. I believe that the Church has an obligation to denounce such breaches of confidentiality and lack of respect for the people who are being served.

Ethical issues related to preventing the sexual transmission of HIV

Since the most common means of HIV spread is through sexual intercourse, perhaps the most controversial and crucial ethical

---

14 US Catholic Bishops' Administrative Board, 1987, *The Many Faces of AIDS*.

issue related to preventing the spread of HIV regards the propriety of means to reduce the risk of transmission during such activity. When scientists proposed that the correct use of a good quality, latex condom could reduce the risk of HIV transmission during sexual intercourse, a great deal of public interest was generated in promoting this means of protection. Unfortunately, many early preventive education efforts focused almost exclusively on this technique and falsely portrayed it as '100% guaranteed safe sex'. They failed to mention that the most effective means to prevent sexual transmission of HIV is abstinence before marriage and sexual fidelity between uninfected partners within marriage – an approach that has long-standing resonance within the teaching and tradition of the Catholic Church.

Catholic and other religious leaders protested against the massive promotion of condoms. Their objections included concerns about promoting sexual activity outside marriage and, not surprisingly for many, became linked to the Church's prohibition of artificial contraception. The strong and public positions taken by the Church against promoting condom use have led to a mistaken perception among AIDS educators, some governments, many health-care professionals and the media that the Catholic Church is obstructing HIV and AIDS prevention efforts and therefore might be a 'promoter of death'. The fact is that the Catholic Church sponsors some excellent educational programmes designed to prevent the sexual transmission of HIV. Curricula have been developed for all levels of Catholic education – to help young people learn about their bodies, about the drive to develop strong and even intimate relationships with others, and about the need to develop discipline and maturity in those relationships so that they will not become manipulative or exploitative. The most consistent message of such education programmes is that sexual activity is to be restricted to faithful marriages, and abstinence can and should be practised outside marriage. Thus Pope John Paul II told young people during his visit to Uganda in February 1993: 'Do not let yourselves be led astray by those who ridicule your chastity or your power to control yourselves. The strength of your future married love depends on the strength of your present effort to learn about true love. Chastity is the only safe and virtuous means to put an end to the tragic plague of AIDS.'[15]

Research findings on HIV prevention education reaffirm traditional church teaching

Over and above the Church's teaching on sexual activity, it is interesting to note recent research findings that clearly indicate that multi-pronged approaches to HIV prevention education are much more effective than programmes that exclusively promote the use of condoms.

'Partner reduction' has been identified as the single greatest factor in reducing HIV/AIDS prevalence in Uganda, with an estimated 65% decline in the numbers of people reporting non-regular partners between 1989 and 1995. In 1989, levels of non-regular partners in Uganda were similar to those in Kenya, Zambia and Malawi. However, by the mid-1990s, non-regular partners were significantly lower (60%) in Uganda compared to these other countries. To a large extent, this discrepancy in terms of partner reduction accounts for the subsequent declines in HIV prevalence in Uganda as well as for the sustained high prevalence of its neighbours. In Thailand, another much-heralded success story, sharp reduction in visits to commercial sex workers and in sexual contact with other non-regular partners contributed greatly to the decline in HIV prevalence.[16]

Similar evidence has been demonstrated with regard to delay in onset of sexual activity. UNAIDS studies in Zambia, Tanzania and Côte d'Ivoire have demonstrated that young people who delay their first sexual encounter have a lower number of pre-marital partners. A study done in Uganda has shown that, in that country, young people between the ages of

15 *Documentation Catholique*, 2068, 21 March 1993, p. 262.

16 'Factors Stabilising HIV Prevalence Rates', abstract presented by Matt Hanley MPH at Family Life Federation Biennial Conference, South Africa, 25 April 2004.

15 and 19, both male and female, have nearly doubled self-reports that they have maintained their virginity.[17]

Contrary indications are evident with regard to prevention campaigns that emphasize condom use. According to an exhaustive review of efforts to promote condom use for HIV prevention in the developing world, there are no examples of prevention campaigns relying primarily on condoms that have reversed any generalized epidemic. Furthermore, the countries with the highest condom use rates – and concomitantly highest rates of artificial contraception – also have some of the highest HIV prevalence rates in the world.[18]

This evidence offers compelling scientific support for our traditional church teaching and thus should further motivate Catholic educators and those engaged in pastoral ministry to promote appropriate, locally inspired interventions that strengthen the family, reinforce healthy norms, protect youth – and especially young women – and encourage abstinence and mutual fidelity in an effective and sustainable manner.

---

17 As reported by D. Wilson, University of Zimbabwe.
18 'Factors Stabilising HIV Prevalence Rates'.

3. Theology in a Time of AIDS

ENDA MCDONAGH

The short if substantial story of the AIDS/HIV pandemic and the comparatively slight story of the Caritas Internationalis group's activity provoke in the telling and re-telling reflection on the Christian traditions which sustain and inspire the group. The re-telling and the reflection result in a re-reading of the Christian scriptures and traditions which may reveal omissions or misunderstandings or at least open the way to fresh and fuller understanding. Liberation theologies of the Latin American, black and feminist kinds are only the most recent examples of how serious social challenges, with their new questions on human meanings and morals, have compelled serious and fruitful re-reading of these scriptures and traditions. It would be rash to claim at this stage at any rate that AIDS/HIV could have far-reaching implications for the practice of theology and the understanding of Christian faith. The experience of liberation theologies should, however, alert us to underestimating the impact of the pandemic on Christian thinking and practice, and above all preclude reducing the discussion to marginal if genuinely important details like the use of condoms or exchange of needles in programmes of prevention. The questions for theology raised by AIDS/HIV may not be confined within the conventional limits of moral theology. Their questions for moral theology go well beyond the tabloid writers' concerns with condoms and needles. (The tabloid mentality is not always restricted to journalists.) The theological re-reading undertaken here examines central issues of Christian belief and living before it takes up some of the significant details in their proper Christian context.

Theology is first of all about God. Discussion of theology in a time of AIDS must begin with God. It is plausible to hold that the pandemic raises no new questions about God, and indeed, as Leslie Houlden argues, no new theological questions at all. At least it raises some old questions in new, and, for the persons immediately involved, in very acute forms. The book of Job may constitute the most profound reflection we have on the relation between human suffering and divine presence in power. Indeed Job's own bodily sufferings and attendant mental anguish and anger may awaken painful echoes in contemporary readers wrestling with the impact of AIDS/HIV. Yet new generations of sufferers with a different ethos of religious belief/doubt and personal, cultural or even medical expectations will experience ultimate questions in quite different ways.

Job's confrontation with the mysterious God of the whirlwind, with his claim to creative laying of the foundations of the earth and to the powerful differentation of animal life, leaves him awed and humbled before the presence and power of his creator and vindicator/redeemer. He has won his argument with his confrere comforters. Personal sin is not the cause of his suffering, and he is not being punished by God for such sin. The lesson must be continually repeated and the book of Job read again and again in face of those Christians who still think of human suffering in terms of God's punishment for personal sin and see a particularly apt application of this doctrine in the emergence of AIDS/HIV.

The presence and power of God in the whirlwind do not resolve all the difficulties. They do, however, open us up to the finally mysterious ways of God in Creation and providence. These ways take a radically new turn in Jesus Christ. The power and the presence, whose time (*kairos*) has come in Jesus' proclamation of the Kingdom or reign of God, offer a very different response to human suffering from the whirlwind proclamation. Leaving aside Jesus' own ministry to the sick, to which we will return, we are confronted with the mystery of God entering fully into the human condition, even to the point of taking on human suffering and dying in the passion and death of Jesus Christ. The crucial and cruciform revelation of God's co-suffering (compassion) with human beings in Jesus manifests a new aspect of the mystery we also call love. It is not simply comprehensible to us, but it does reassure us about the presence. 'Where are you God as I am overcome by the pain and desperation?' 'Right here with you just as I was on Calvary.' And the power, the omnipotence, as we used to say? No more absent or frustrated than on Calvary but taking its mysterious ways through creaturely and bodily fragility to a healing in love and life that may or may not issue in renewed bodily life and health. The inexhaustible loving which endured through Calvary does not abandon those for whom Calvary was undertaken in the first place.

Jesus and the Kingdom

Jesus and his God are not to be understood simply in terms of the passion and death on Calvary. These undoubtedly form the climax to his life and mission, as they do to the Gospel narratives. Yet they are only properly and fully understood in the light of Jesus' public life and ministry, by which he pursued his mission and encountered his destiny. By the announcement of the Kingdom or reign of God which opened the ministry and specified the mission, Jesus at once confirmed and transformed the tradition of Israel. The Kingdom motif in Israel anticipated a restoration of a Davidic-style kingdom with the God of Israel, Yahweh, newly present in all his power and glory. The presence in power which Jesus offered in the name of his Father was no less glorious for those with eyes to see, but its paradoxical character defeated the perception of many contemporaries.

This was not a Kingdom first of all for the powerful and wealthy, who were to be toppled from their seats and sent empty away. The sinners and the prostitutes, the poor and the socially marginalized like the lepers and the tax gatherers would go first into the Kingdom. By identifying with these, by eating and drinking with them, Jesus overturned the accepted canons of religious and political respectability. It was eventually to cost him his life as he was considered too subversive of the established order, and after a show trial was crucified between two other criminals outside the gates of the city. Exclusion had reached its terminus in criminalization and execution for him who would make the excluded the centre of his mission. For Christians who feel the urge to reject or avoid or neglect people living with AIDS/HIV, the counter-example of Jesus should be a forceful reminder. As we do it to one of these least ones.

Jesus did not simply seek the company of the excluded, he did see that as a way of establishing a new set of relationships, a new kind of community, a new Israel which would embody the Kingdom of God which he announced. In this new community God's presence and power would be evident above all in the practices of love. And it would be effective love – feeding the hungry, setting the prisoners free, restoring sight to the blind, letting the lame walk, healing all manner of sickness. Jesus' ministry to the sick has inspired generations of Christians. He explicitly rejected the old mistake of Job's comforters. 'Neither this man nor his parents have sinned,' he told his disciples of the man born blind. In this case as in others the healing manifested the power and the glory of God by attending to immediate needs of the suffering and excluded. The new Israel would also be a new creation with the God-given powers of creation restored and fulfilled. In Christian care and human scientific development these God-given resources are to be harnessed in restoration of health and comfort of the afflicted. Love after the manner of Jesus, unconditional acceptance and care of the needy must be expressed in the most effective way possible – medically, socially and personally.

Moral theology and natural law

The community of disciples which follows Jesus and seeks to proclaim and promote his Kingdom of God in the world for the healing and transformation of the world must act in imitation of Jesus, sharing his heart and mind. The reading and re-reading of that mind and its thoughtful application to the needy and excluded of a particular time form that part of the permanent theological task called moral theology or Christian ethics. It is a task that must be approached thoughtfully using the resources of God-given minds after the fashion of Augustine,

Aquinas, Barth and all the other great Christian thinkers. It can never treat the mind in separation from heart and action, but it must be true to its gifts and limitations. Over the millennia Christian, Jewish and indeed pagan minds have contributed powerfully to elucidating how Christians might act individually and socially in imitation of Christ. The more systematic attempts to do this have issued in different if related theologies which were distinguished at a later period in the Catholic tradition (*c.*1600) as moral theology. It has never been an entirely satisfactory distinction, particularly when it hardened into sharp division. It was a distinction unknown to Augustine and Aquinas. Here the focus will be on some systematic outline of Christian living according to the mind of Christ, without losing touch with the biblical narratives or later doctrinal insights and developments.

Catholic moral theology has been dominated over the centuries by the concept of natural law. With a certain biblical basis and a strong base in the Western philosophical tradition it has proved of enormous value both in the development of systematic thinking about Christian morals and in dealing with particular cases. In Caritas Internationalis' ventures into areas of very limited Christian background in Asia and Africa this same natural law approach offered a first step, if only a first, in seeking some mutual moral understanding on AIDS/HIV with people of quite different religious and cultural backgrounds. For Catholics and people sharing a similar philosophical background it will continue to sustain and illuminate moral analysis. The absence of what Alasdair MacIntyre might term any public moral consensus can make the claims made for natural law from a church or theological background seem arbitrary or simply the diktats of authority without any real basis in the reason to which it pretends. The current criticisms of the Enlightenment enthronement of reason make natural law arguments harder to sustain outside a limited Catholic circle. The approach adopted here is not therefore directly based on natural law arguments – the sources are more immediately biblical and theological. Yet it will undoubtedly overlap with and be nourished by the content of the natural law tradition in its structural design and case discussion.

47

Kingdom values and moral virtues

The new presence and power of God realized in the life and ministry, death and resurrection of Jesus Christ is another description of the Kingdom of God which he declared fulfilled in his time (*kairos*), fulfilled that is in relation to the promises his people of Israel had received and the expectations they had developed: a paradoxical and disconcerting fulfilment, as we have seen. Fuller and further descriptions of the Kingdom may be drawn from Jesus' teaching and ministry, as well as from his death and resurrection and his immediate disciples' response. However, even a cursory reading of Jesus' parables of the Kingdom reveals how obscure or rather mysterious it remains. Inevitably so when one is speaking of the presence and power of God, creating and sustaining, enabling and healing, fulfilling and transforming humanity and the cosmos, to essay a further but still beggarly description of the mystery which we inhabit and which inhabits us.

The Kingdom of God which is about us and within us, in Jesus' own words, seeks and enables our recognition, our expression and manifestation of it, our participation in its development. As we are called in the Genesis narrative to participate in God's original creative activity, so we are called in the Jesus narrative to participate in God's new creative activity. But who are the 'we' who are called? The 'we' must match the range of Creation and new creation. The 'we' is first and last of all humankind. It is only the community of Jesus' disciples who can explicitly recognize the Kingdom. But the Kingdom is for all human beings, and above all by Jesus' example and teaching for the least of our human sisters and brothers, meaning the least by the standards of the worldly world, the poor, the socially excluded, the sick, who in a time and place of AIDS can so easily coincide. So the disciples of Jesus, as entrusted with the vision and enabling call of the Kingdom, must offer a lead in responding to these least ones by active caring, loving personal relationships and structural reform.

The anticipation of Jesus' vision of God's Kingdom which the Hebrew prophets in particular proclaimed provides a basis for a moral structuring of the Kingdom call as it affects the

Christian lives of disciples and the moral goals of the whole human community. While this is primarily a biblical and theological approach, it will have evident connections with a natural law approach. It is not the only biblical/theological approach possible, but it may be quite illuminating in relating morally the Kingdom of God to human society in this time of AIDS/HIV.

As I have already developed the discussion of Kingdom values more fully elsewhere I will deal rather briefly with them here. Within the biblical–theological tradition it is possible to discern a range of values which are to be realized in the presence and through the power of God. Some of these express the presence and power of Godself in stories of Israel and of Jesus. Characteristic of God in covenant they are to characterize human beings in covenant with one another as well as with God. They embody the very presence and power of God in personal interaction and social structure. In that created and creative dialectic of person and society, Kingdom values foreshadow fulfilment of person and society, the thrust of God's successive covenants. The realization of these values, however partial, is a realization of the Kingdom in its historical limitations. In another philosophical idiom they may provide a basis for a vision of society which connects with traditions other than the Jewish and Christian.

The four Kingdom values which seem to serve these theological and philosophical purposes are those of truth, freedom, justice and peace (*shalom*). They may also be called primary Kingdom values because they reflect the primary reality of God. Other values which do not reflect God immediately may be termed secondary. This does not make them unimportant but simply states that they are not in themselves characteristic of God. Values related to our embodied condition such as chastity are not directly applicable to God and so are secondary in this sense.

Presence and power of God in truth

The pursuit of Pilate's question, 'What is truth?' in its current hermeneutical complexities is a task for another time and place. Truth is central to the Jewish and Christian traditions, as central as God. It *is* God. More accurately and profoundly, God is truth. The ultimate reality revealing itself is basic truth for humanity, at once summoning and enabling human beings to recognize the truth and to live by it. Only by listening to the God-given call to truth, by seeking and at least partially attaining the truth and striving to do it or live by it, can human beings live with one another. The dialectic of person and society demands minimal truthfulness for its minimal successful resolution. Such minimal achievement is an expression of the Kingdom, of the presence and power of God.

Social and personal crises like war and the pandemic AIDS/HIV threaten truth. At least without continuous commitment to truth, the crisis will be misunderstood and the response mistaken. The temptation to conceal the truth of the extent of the pandemic is one aspect of how the threat may aggravate the crisis. Fears of contagion by family, friends and carers based on untruth can readily undermine social and personal responses. Only the truth in the Gospel phrase will set us free to deal effectively with the crisis. And it is the divinely begotten hunger for truth which may hope through research to find medical means of prevention and cure.

Quite complex problems of confidentiality and information can arise for people living with AIDS/HIV, for their partners and carers, medical and social. How the truth is respected in the context of personal rights to privacy and dignity and of social need may not be easily discerned. The other Kingdom values of freedom, justice and peace/solidarity will play a role here, as they will in handling most moral dilemmas arising from the pandemic. Beyond that it is important to recognize that Kingdom values do not come cheaply. Truth, like grace, will often be costly. It is the responsibility of the community of disciples, of witnesses to the Kingdom, to ensure with Jesus Christ that the cost is shared and the heavier burden of it borne by those in the best position to pay.

Presence and power of God in freedom

The freedom of God in creation and covenant forms the basis of human freedom of choice as well as of the progressive liberation of person and society which the Kingdom of God seeks, enables and achieves, if only partially in history. In the messianic programme announced by Jesus in Luke 4 the basis of Kingdom liberation is already set. With prisoners to go free, the blind to see, the lame to walk and the poor to receive the good news of the Kingdom, the basic enslavements of the human condition – personal and social, sacred and profane in sin and oppression – are to be overcome. The freedom of the children of God is at once gift and task. The maturing of person and society so that each person and each society is gradually enabled to harness itself and its resources in creative self-expression and other-service indicates the human shape of Kingdom liberation.

In face of the pandemic, the search for freedom from further infection through effective and humane preventive measures is an essential response to the Kingdom call. Development of therapeutic measures connects the Kingdom call to truth and its call to free people from the slavery of disease. And freedoms may well clash here – or certainly appear to clash. Programmes of mandatory testing for so-called risk groups or of quarantine for people with AIDS/HIV are usually unfair restriction of people already restricted socially or physically. Here the cross-over between freedom and justice emerges in human rights or liberties. In quite a different manner, freedom and maturity emerge for the sexually active as forming the basis for the integration of sexuality into personal maturity in relating to other sexual beings. The interrelation of the primary Kingdom values with one another and their influence in shaping the secondary values must be continually kept in mind.

Presence and power of God in justice

For many biblical scholars, justice is the central description of God in the scriptures, particularly in the Hebrew scriptures. A more popular but inaccurate analysis would contrast the God of justice in the Hebrew scriptures and covenant with the

God of love in the Christian scriptures and new covenant. In both scriptures the justice of God is the shape which the love of God, or better, the love that is God, takes in covenantal saving relationship with the errant Israel and sinful humanity.

Divine justice characterizes God's commitment to and responsibility for the world and for humanity through the covenants of creation, with Abraham and Moses, and in Jesus Christ. That commitment and responsibility require and enable human commitment and responsibility to and for one another. The great prophets of justice in eighth-century Israel (BCE) denounced as unacceptable to God assemblies of worshippers who neglected the widow, the orphan and the stranger, the judges who refused justice to the poor (cf. Amos). For Jeremiah, faith in God is primarily expressed in justice. In more contemporary language recognition of, respect for and response to the human others is the test of authentic recognition of the ultimate other. The fairness and equality which justice demands focuses in both Old and New Testament versions of God's Kingdom on the deprived and excluded. The blessed who hunger and thirst after justice as disciples of Jesus will be judged, rendered justice themselves on how far they fed and cared for these least ones. To feed and care for them is to care for Jesus, the incarnate ultimate other.

In a more analytic mode justice is distinguished as personal and social, as regulating fairness in relations between individual persons and in structural relations within society. Many of the problems revealed by the pandemic are problems of justice, personal and social. Some of these may be adequately expressed in terms of human rights and pursued in that fashion. However, not all delicate justice problems may be translated into human rights language without considerable loss of moral impact. Issues of testing, for example, may be usefully treated in terms of rights but there are cases such as mandatory testing of candidates for admission to seminaries and religious orders where larger concerns like witness may also need consideration. Here the interconnection between Kingdom values emerges as freedom and justice overlap in rights, and truth and peace overlap in witness.

Presence and power of God in peace

Peace is a much neglected theme in theology, and particularly in moral theology, where it barely figured as a side issue in the just-war discussion. Yet it is a central theme in the biblical tradition of the Kingdom and increasingly central to the survival of the human race. The presence and power of God to be realized and manifest in genuine peace between and within individuals, between and within societies, constitutes the most profound Kingdom challenge facing the disciples of Jesus Christ today. In the biblical tradition peace, *shalom* in Hebrew, far exceeds the minimalist absence of war or maintenance of law and order, the *pax romana*. Flourishing in communion might be a much better description of the peace anticipated in the Kingdom and offered by Jesus to his disciples and through them to the world. It incorporates both ideas of flourishing in unity or solidarity with implications of truth, freedom and justice. It also involves the more specifically Christian themes of healing, reconciliation and forgiveness.

The AIDS/HIV pandemic should stimulate then a much-needed development in understanding and promoting the Kingdom value of peace. The dimensions of solidarity, healing, reconciling and forgiving have obvious relevance for both the personal and social challenges of AIDS/HIV. Their understanding and application here will provide insight into other peace needs and possibilities.

Kingdom values and sexuality

The presence and power of God which Jesus announced as the Kingdom involves personal, social and cosmic transformation. In seeking to express in moral terms the significance of the Kingdom, four structural values were selected as primary for their biblical roots, their structural role in moral living and above all their attribution to Godself in Hebrew and Christian tradition. Other moral values which by these criteria are described as secondary have their own biblical roots, their role in moral living and a relationship, however indirect, to God.

Yet the primary values will shape these secondary values in ways to be explored. Of immediate concern here is the value associated with sexuality, the value of chastity and how it is influenced by the primary values.

That God was not sexually described or defined was a notable and distinctive achievement of Hebrew religion. However, the origins and development of human sexuality were related by that tradition in its own distinctive way to God's creative presence and power. In one Genesis account (Genesis 1) when God created humanity, 'male and female he created (it), in the image of God he created them'. For love and companionship, for life-giving and co-creating, this gift of sexual duality was given to humans as images of God. This kind of human loving, sexual loving, is celebrated in itself as gift in the Song of Songs. In other biblical writings it is recognized as mirroring God's love for Israel (Hosea, Isaiah) and as a sacrament or sign of Christ's love for the Church, the community of his disciples. A Christian theological view of sexuality has no place for the 'sex is dirty' syndrome.

The divine gift of sexuality implies a human call and task. The goals of loving and life-giving, broader human goals are specified more exactly in sexuality. These goals have to be sought over time by the development and integration of a person's sexual endowment into a fuller personal, relational and social life. The Catholic and Christian tradition with its biblical foundation sees the climax of that development emerging in marriage. Full sexual expression of the whole person belongs in this tradition to the established and yet developing community of love of one man and one woman which is open to new life. The Kingdom value of truth, with its associates of fidelity and honesty, belongs to and protects this sacramental community, as the Catholic tradition describes it. Freedom is essential to the origins of such a commitment, as the freedom interrogation at the beginning of the marriage rite confirms. Justice belongs in different ways to the fulfilment of the marriage call. The injustice element in adultery provides one example of this. Without peace and its unitive, reconciling and forgiving dimensions, marriage would not exist or survive.

The Christian community and the Catholic Church also

recognize the sexual endowment and Kingdom call of the unmarried, the single, the celibate and the widowed. Indeed, celibacy for the sake of the Kingdom has played a significant, sometimes a dominating, role in relating Kingdom and sexuality. The 'perfect' chastity of the celibate calling was contrasted with the 'imperfect' of marriage. Celibates and other unmarried people are not asexual and not automatically and statically chaste. Chastity is not something a person is born with and with a bit of luck hangs on to. No moral value or associated virtue is like that. People become chaste, as indicated above, by gradually integrating their sexual gifts into responses appropriate to the different relationships in their lives, husband–wife, parent–child, brother–sister, friends, neighbours, colleagues, acquaintances. So celibates and other unmarried people are called to grow into the value and virtue of chastity. In this growth the primary Kingdom values will protect and promote the value of chastity for the unmarried as they do for married people. It must be admitted, however, that little specific positive elaboration for growth into chastity by the unmarried exists in the Christian moral tradition. Moral theologians and teachers have usually settled for the simple negative guidelines – no intercourse outside marriage. Reducing the whole sexual life to intercourse is not particularly helpful to married people either. Celibates and singles, heterosexual and homosexual, need more help than that if they are to become dynamically chaste. They too are called to be people whose sexuality promotes loving and life-giving, enriching relationships as signs and realizations of the presence and power of God. Some further consideration will be given to this in the later sections.

Christian ministry and morality

With the biblical–theological background sketched here and in the context of the ministry promoted by Caritas Internationalis in response to the pandemic, it may help to focus the discussion of practical moral issues in terms of Christian ministry. In this way particular issues are related to the personal ministry of Jesus in the Gospels, and to the ministry of the community of disciples in discerning and promoting the Kingdom, with their emphasis on the deprived and excluded. The moral distortions which Jesus criticized for imposing insupportable burdens on the weak may be more readily apparent and avoided.

Companionship

Jesus' recognition and inclusion, to the point of table-fellowship, of the poor and excluded, provides the model for Christian ministry to people with AIDS/HIV. The first moral response of disciples must be to accompany the ill and infected. Without unconditional acceptance and persistent accompaniment, the most skilful professional care, moral analysis and education will lack Christian authenticity.

Companionship (like sharing bread–table companionship) will only persist if the suffering is shared. This remark needs careful unpacking. Clearly one human person cannot fully understand the suffering of another and so share adequately even at the simply knowing level. Much less can one person take over or share in a direct physical way another's pain. Yet sympathy and compassion are more than simple companionship or care. Indeed, companionship and care are stimulated and sustained by the acceptance of the other in her suffering into one's heart and mind and imagination. Despite the limitations of language we can say that we are sometimes inhabited by the others, by the suffering of the others. This compassionate reception of deprived human others is at the heart of Jesus' ministry. God's acceptance, being inhabited in Jesus by the burdens and pain, privations and failures (sins) of all human beings, is at the heart of the doctrine of salvation. In imitation of Jesus and of the Father, disciples open themselves to the suffering others while respecting their distinctiveness as persons even in their suffering. The patronizing encouragement of dependency fails to respect the suffering person from whom the carer has so much to receive. Companionship is at the service of the others' personal self-respect, integrity and autonomy. Compassionate companionship after the manner of Jesus and God, which involves co-creating, co-suffering and co-redeeming in the community of caring, may be the best description of

the first moral obligation of disciples to people living with
AIDS/HIV.

Care

To be true to itself, compassionate companionship must seek to
offer effective care to the suffering while encouraging and
enabling them to care for themselves as far as possible. Given
the limitations of their freedom, justice also demands such
caring. Only in this way can they be integrated into the healing
solidarity and peace of the Kingdom. Care, like compassion and
all other aspects of ministry, must constantly look for guidance
to these primary Kingdom values.

Care must operate at every level at which suffering operates
and not be reduced simply to medical care, essential as that is.
At the medical level itself the call to truth in researching further
understanding of the origins, transmission and overcoming
of the virus(es) has obvious Kingdom resonances. A further
Kingdom call is to ensure that medical understanding is effectively disseminated, particularly where myths about origin and
transmission are widespread. Sometimes these myths are simply
due to ignorance. Sometimes they are promoted out of preju-
dice/ prejudgement about so-called 'deviants' such as gay men
or drug users while information about heterosexual transmission is ignored or distorted.

Research into cause and cure is still so far from completion
that it must be encouraged and funded as fully as possible.
Meantime, the best medical care available must be provided as
truthfully, as freely and as fairly or justly as possible. The
manipulation of sufferers by deception or coercion in the name
of treatment clearly violates personal dignity and Kingdom
values. Financial exploitation by medical and pharmaceutical
interests is no less morally objectionable. Striving for fair distribution of therapies available becomes a particular Christian
responsibility in a world where the powerful and privileged
readily corner medical as well as other resources, and the generally deprived, especially in the developing world, are exposed
to the worst ravages of the disease.

Medical treatment, even much more effective treatment than

is at present available, could not hope on its own to heal the psychological and social destruction wrought by AIDS/HIV. Counselling care remains critical to psychological healing. Social healing involves more radical measures, from overcoming prejudice to cultural change to economic reform. Programmes of care in these different areas, which for Christians form part of the coming of the Kingdom, will be effective only over time. The Kingdom is coming, but in history only over time. This may be illustrated by one or two instances.

To care effectively for drug users, already infected with HIV or exposed to infection, takes time. Drug addiction is not cured instantly and by a simple decision of the will. Willingness to be helped will usually be very hard to elicit or to encourage. In the time needed for that, an important first step in saving life and making time for recovery could be weaning people from the use of shared needles. In the impoverished circumstances in which so many drug addicts live, it may be necessary, among other measures, to provide clean needles free of charge, without endorsing in any way drug addiction or the drug culture. A Christian care of drug addicts, which seeks to protect the infected from infecting others, and the non-infected from being infected by others, could regard the provision of clean needles as a morally acceptable interim measure, where the interim is being used to save life and so offers some hope of tackling and eventually overcoming the drug addiction and the drug culture.

In quite different situations of AIDS/HIV transmission by sexual intercourse, prostitutes and their clients in sex tourism and the sex industry may be no more capable of instant conversion than drug addicts. This 'incapacity' has its psychological reasons, which vary with individual people. Social, cultural and economic reasons, which may be even stronger, vary with the particular society and culture. Some studies as well as popular impressions suggest that for prostitutes economic reasons may be strongest of all. To care for people with AIDS/ HIV in these situations and as part of that care to prevent them spreading it further, every dimension of the problem has to be analysed and tackled. All this demands time for individuals and groups. In that time, care for life may require interim measures akin to the provision of clean needles for drug addicts. With all the risks of misunderstanding both in regard to the 'safety' of so-called safe sex and to the apparent endorsement of promiscuity, it may be socially necessary and morally legitimate to accept the use of condoms. However, it must be made clear that this is in no way regarded as good in itself. It is tolerated as an interim measure to protect life and allow time for the personal and social conversion which the coming of the Kingdom calls for and enables in these situations also.

4. AIDS and Responsibility

CHARLES RYAN

The word 'responsibility' has three important levels of meaning in the context of the Christian Church dealing with the AIDS pandemic in Southern Africa:

1 Who or what is responsible for the AIDS pandemic?
2 What is the responsibility of an individual AIDS sufferer?
3 What is the responsibility of the Church in the presence of AIDS?

Who or what is responsible for AIDS?

To know the origins of HIV/AIDS is important in the context of finding a cure and prevention. If, as is often suggested, the infection transferred from monkeys or another animal species, the knowledge of this fact would help research scientists identify where to focus their attentions so as to know, for example, why monkeys do not themselves develop the symptoms of AIDS while carrying the virus. Furthermore, if, as would emerge in another theory of origins, the virus is the result of a genetic accident in a laboratory where bacteria and viruses were being studied, that knowledge would provide a starting point for finding how to cure and prevent. There is a third notion that is circulating in some circles,[1] that AIDS is a weapon used by a

---

1 In an unpublished survey conducted in 1997 at the University of Uyo, Akwa Ibom State, Nigeria, to which 400 undergraduates responded, 65% of the respondents indicated that they believed that AIDS was a disease either

minority to further their aims. Ridiculous as it may seem to some, it still finds a place in the discussion of 'Who is responsible for AIDS?'

However, the frequency of this questioning is not because of its scientific usefulness, but because of the desire of the immature[2] human personality to apportion blame so as to escape from the need to accept personal or social responsibility. Superficially, the logic leads to blaming God, especially as the proportions of the epidemic become such that they can be described as 'out of control'. It is theologically correct to say that God, who is all powerful, could have prevented humanity from being afflicted with this calamity, or, now that for humanly unfathomable reasons God caused or allowed it to happen, could listen to our prayers and cause a cure to be found.

Let us immediately dispose of the notion that God is careless of the sufferings of humanity. The idea that God inflicted humanity with AIDS recalls the Existentialists' questions: 'Can a God who permitted the holocaust to happen exist?' or 'Can a God who permitted Hiroshima to happen exist?' The Existentialists answered the question by deciding that if such a god exists then God is irrelevant to humanity. Nevertheless this question is important when dealing with the Fundamentalists' assertion that AIDS is a punishment from God.

There is a certain simplistic attractiveness in the notion that God is punishing humankind for the sexual promiscuity that is rife in our age. There is also the unquestionable fact that the spread of AIDS has been facilitated by promiscuous sexual activity, and could be contained if sexual activity were limited to faithful monogamous relationships. To see AIDS, therefore, as a punishment for humankind's departure from what Christianity and other religions have always taught about sex being

---

used by the white race to prevent black people from progressing, or used by 'religious people' to prevent young people from enjoying the fruits of their liberation. This should be set against a further minority view that AIDS does not actually exist.

2 Immaturity being a state that is much more common than humanity would like to admit.

exclusively for marriage, appears to have some merit. The breakdown of the extremely rigid discipline about sexual matters that was exercised by virtually all traditional religions could equally be seen as pointing to AIDS as an indication of the anger of the 'gods' or the spirits of the forefathers.

However, the established Christian churches have been unanimous in condemning the idea of a vindictive God. The Catholic Bishops of Southern Africa are unambiguous: 'AIDS must never be seen as a punishment from God.'[3] As early as 1986 Richard Holloway (at a time when AIDS was identified with homosexual activity), the Anglican Archbishop of Edinburgh, dealt eloquently with the so-called 'wrath of God' of the Fundamentalists:

> To argue that AIDS is God's punishment on homosexuals seems to me to be morally repugnant and illogical. Morally repugnant, because it creates a picture of God as an enraged terrorist who fashions and throws bombs at his enemies, no matter who gets injured. But it is also illogical, because it is inconsistent. It differentiates between male and female homo-sexuals, and seems to put the God who inspires scientific research against the God who dreams up new diseases in his great laboratory in the sky. But if it is argued that God does reward wickedness so specifically, why is he taking so long to lob something at rapists or child abusers, groups that are infinitely more malign in their effects than most gay men?[4]

Catholics may claim that they do not subscribe to the blatant 'wrath of God' theory, but might well be guilty of a more subtle version. Kenneth Kearon sums up the 'more-gentle-punishing-God' approach:

> [the angry punishing God image] was not the response of the main churches, whose statements, especially in the early

---

3 'A Message of Hope', statement from the Plenary Session of the Southern African Catholic Bishops' Conference [SACBC], Pretoria, 30 July 2001.

4 K. Kearon, 1999, *Medical Ethics – An Introduction*, Dublin: Columba Press, p. 118.

stages, often followed a similar pattern: an expression of genuine compassion, a call for adequate medical and research resources to be made available, and then there usually followed a re-affirmation of traditional Christian attitudes to sexual relationships and drug abuse and a warning that only by accepting Christian standards in these areas could the disease be avoided. This latter section is certainly not 'wrath of God' language, but there is a strong undercurrent of 'we warned you', 'we were right all along' in this sort of response. It is implicitly saying 'something bad will happen to you unless you follow Christian standards'. AIDS is the consequence of not following the Christian way.[5]

The image of an angry God appears to be absent in that position, but nevertheless there is a picture of a creating God who will arrange for dire consequences to follow if we do not respect the rules he has given. If we look at the position taken by the Southern African Bishops and many individual bishops in this geographical area, are we not looking at an exact replica of what Kearon discusses? We might be avoiding and condemning the idea of an angry punishing God, but by constantly putting AIDS into a moral context we fall into the trap of implying that God has made laws that, if they are ignored, will bring the direst consequences – AIDS being a good example. No doubt promiscuous sexual activity does have serious consequences for the individuals concerned, and society in general, but hinting that God wills that AIDS should be among those consequences is surely not Christian.

The fact is that God has not inflicted humankind with AIDS. Whatever the origin of AIDS – be it an accident or the result of ignorance or malice – it must be seen, if it is an accident, in the same light as an unexpected destructive storm or a widespread drought that causes starvation or some such enormous tragedy, and if it is the result of the malice or stupidity of humans, it can be compared to a major war or civil strife. Did we blame God for the 'El Nino' weather phenomenon, or for apartheid or

---

5 Kearon, *Medical Ethics*, p. 117.

World War II? (The fact that the legal profession refers to natural disasters as 'Acts of God' is a graphic illustration of the fact that popular notions of religion can be very misleading.) The one difference is that the AIDS tragedy is of such a magnitude that we can truly say that humankind has never seen the likes before. The need to distance the Church from the 'angry punishing God' and the 'We told you so' attitude is critical. It must be done energetically and repeatedly at every level of the Church's presence, bearing in mind that we are part of a Judeo-Christian tradition that portrayed a Jahweh who 'punished' Adam and Eve with banishment, Sodom and Gomorrah with destruction, the people of Noah's time with inundation, and the idolatrous kingdom of Israel with captivity. So we must remind ourselves first, and repeatedly remind others, that we are in a new dispensation. It has been revealed to us in Christ that the only God who exists is a loving Father who is kind and merciful, '. . . For God sent his Son into the world, not to judge the world, but so that through him the world might be saved . . .' (John 3.17). It must, however, be noted that from the beginning our own Christian tradition has been plagued by dualism, Puritanism in its various manifestations, and a belief that celibacy is inherently superior to the married state. Sexuality was perceived as a very 'dangerous' phenomenon, not least by the celibate leadership of the Church!

The responsibility of an individual AIDS sufferer

There is a second level of responsibility that arises regularly. That is when we find ourselves asking why a particular person became HIV-positive. Recently I asked a group of seminarians and religious that I was teaching what their first response was when hearing that someone was HIV-positive. The chorused answer was: 'How did he get it?' Subsequently, when I was discussing with a group of priests how difficult I was finding it to get students to stop thinking in terms of guilt when confronting AIDS, they became very silent until one of them said: 'But, are they [AIDS sufferers] not guilty?'

It cannot be denied that the Church has always taught that

sexual activity is for married people only.[6] The vast majority of Catholics could hardly claim ignorance of this teaching. If we find statements from the Church recommending that we do not judge AIDS sufferers, they are usually associated with the view that 'after all, AIDS can also be contracted by blood transfusion, and by an infant from its mother etc.' but it is somehow implied that those who contracted AIDS by extra-marital sexual activity are guilty! This is another view that must be actively and energetically opposed.

The Church teaches that serious sin requires grave matter, full knowledge and full consent. There has also been a strong moral teaching that in the area of sexuality all matter was 'grave'.[7] But even if we were to accept the latter teaching, one must look seriously at the other traditional 'ingredients' for serious sin – full knowledge and full consent.

A generation ago the Church refused Christian burial to those who committed suicide. This policy has been abandoned, not because suicide is now accepted as moral, but because psychology has taught the Church that the vast majority of suicides are committed by people who are under such pressure of fear and despair that they are actually incapable of 'knowing what they do', and therefore deserve sympathy and not condemnation. The possibility of such situations destroying or reducing 'culpability' has always been a feature of Catholic moral theology, but it is only of late that the Church realized the extent that they feature, at least in suicide. Psychology has also pointed out the degree to which freedom and consent are compromised for many people in the area of their sexuality, especially when confronted with the aggressive promotion of promiscuous sexual activity that is part of their environment, as well as social and economic circumstances:

---

6 The Catechism of the Catholic Church says: 'Fornication is carnal union between an unmarried man and an unmarried woman. It is gravely contrary to the dignity of persons and of human sexuality which is naturally ordered to the good of spouses and the generation and education of children' (p. 543 of the 1994 Ibadan/Nairobi English translation).

7 One cannot identify a time when this teaching was abandoned, but in the post-Vatican age the notion seems to have died a natural death.

. . . a young person may grow up in a traditional African family, which is also devoutly Catholic, attend an urban school with students of diverse backgrounds, regularly watch and identify with American TV and movies, and belong to a soccer club with other young men. It is likely and possible that each of these contexts may be informed by quite different and even irreconcilable values and attitudes about sexuality, its meaning and its control. It is in the face of these competing contexts and value systems that young people have to make choices about their sexuality and sexual behaviour.[8]

To assume that every member of the Church knows that the Catholic teaching comes from God and therefore must supersede all other values is surely presumptuous, considering the work of Piaget, Kohlberg and others who have stressed the inability of immature people to make independent choices based on principles. The same empirical data have also illustrated the fact that a very high percentage of humanity never reaches moral maturity and therefore will always conform to the conventions of the environment upon which they are emotionally dependent.

So, without having to deny that extra-marital sexual activity is harmful to society, inimical to the possibility of real commitment and contrary to the beauty of God's creative will, all the indications are that the vast majority of Christians living in South Africa may be involved in objectively immoral, sexual activity, but are not guilty because of defects in knowledge, freedom or ability to give proper consent in matters of sexuality. If there is any moral guilt in this matter it must surely be found in the failure of church communities to communicate to their members an authentic appreciation of the beauty of chastity and a supportive environment where it can be lived in joy. Merely to repeat that sexual activity outside marriage is sinful will simply not work, or as Lindegger and van Rooyen put it: 'Early strategies focused on individual decision making

---

8 G. Lindegger and H. van Rooyen, from an unpublished working paper of the Theological Advisory Committee of the SACBC, 2002.

about sexuality, and attempted to get people to change their behaviour through messages of fear and guilt. The evidence is that these strategies have been largely unsuccessful.'[9]

Kevin T. Kelly, a respected English Catholic moral theologian, reaches the same conclusion in a different way in advocating a 'person-centred' sexual ethic, saying:

> . . . a sexual ethic for to-day needs to listen to what is going on among young people. Many feel so alienated from the world of so-called responsible adults that they are trying to find some sense of identity in their youth culture. And casual sex is part of that youth culture.[10]

He points out that 'individual moral agents are not all proceeding from the same starting-point'.[11]

This issue could also be approached from the point of view of the notion of Conscience. The Second Vatican Council made a clear statement:

> But that which is truly freedom is an exceptional sign of the image of God in man. For God willed that man should 'be left in the hand of his own counsel' (Sirach 15.14) so that he might of his own accord seek his creator and freely attain his full and blessed perfection by cleaving to him. Man's dignity, therefore, requires him to act out of conscious and free choice, as moved and drawn in a personal way from within, and not by blind impulses in himself or by mere external constraint.[12]

Duska and Whelan comment on that passage:

> Is not the post-conciliar Church, in effect, telling people that although it can give moral guidance, it cannot make up

---

9 Lindegger and van Rooyen, unpublished working paper.

10 K. T. Kelly, 1998, *New Directions in Sexual Ethics: Moral Theology and the Challenge of AIDS*, London: Geoffrey Chapman, p. 185.

11 Kelly, *New Directions*, p. 187.

12 A. Flannery (ed.), 1975, *The Church in the Modern World*, 17, Dublin: Vatican Council II, p. 917.

people's minds for them? Does it not insist that mature Christianity demands that people take responsibility for their own moral decisions? How then can the striving for autonomy be unorthodox?[13]

Imagine parents saying to their teenage son: 'We wish you would not go to Durban during the New Year weekend. It is extremely dangerous on the roads at that time of year. Please stay at home and attend the New Year Vigil in the Church.' But the parents already know that the teenager is bent on going with his peers, and there is no time or suitable environment to make him see the prudence of staying away from Durban. Which would be better to say to the son: (a) 'We forbid you to go to Durban, and if you do go, you are no longer a son of ours!' or (b) 'We wish you would not go, but if you really feel you must go, please do not drink and drive, and always fasten your seat belt, so that the chances of being killed will be drastically reduced'? The going to Durban in that case could be described as immoral and unsuitable for a committed Christian, but the parents can see the realities in the situation and accept the alternative with precautions.

But because of our unease with sexuality (partly caused by the dualistic and puritanical history of the Church and the fact that the leaders are celibates) we find it difficult to handle a similar set of options where sex is involved. Could we imagine ourselves as a Church saying: 'Sexual activity outside marriage is harmful and unsafe, and we wish you did not engage in it, but if you insist on being sexually active outside marriage, please, at least use a condom'? But, if not, why not? In spite of expressed doubts about the efficacy of condoms to prevent the transmission of HIV, there is no doubt that using a condom does afford a degree of protection against this deadly condition. The technical reality is that sex with a condom is safer than sex without a condom – all other things being equal.

In summary, a very high percentage of young people are not guilty of immorality when they are sexually active, by reason

---

13 R. Duska and M. Whelan, 1975, *Moral Development – A Guide to Piaget and Kohlberg*, New York: Paulist Press, p. 91.

of their imperfect knowledge and freedom. Likewise a high percentage of chronologically mature people are not morally mature, and share the adolescents' inability to make an independent moral choice. Third, an authentic notion of conscience allows for the possibility of mature adults taking a practical decision in matters of sexual morality that differs from the ideals proposed by the Church. Even if it were the Church's role to judge ('Judge not, that you may not be judged'), the presumption should be that, in the climate of South African society, the consciences of many people who are sexually active outside marriage are free of guilt. So, even if HIV/AIDS is caused by extra-marital sexual activity, the issue of moral guilt must be put aside. Finally, even if a victim of AIDS admitted moral guilt, there is no relationship between the guilt and the disproportionate affliction that is AIDS.

I find it useful to summarize this position by saying that *no one deserves to have AIDS*!

The responsibility of the Church

We have been told, and it is accepted, that the Catholic Church in Southern Africa is doing more to combat the spread of AIDS and help HIV-positive people and AIDS sufferers than any non-governmental organization. We are also aware that the Church recognizes, and is actively confronting, many social problems in Southern Africa – unemployment, poverty, breakdown of family life, ongoing racism even after the collapse of apartheid. The problems are many and enormous – so much so that many concerned Christians are close to despair. However, the nature and magnitude of the HIV/AIDS pandemic is such that it is in a totally different category from all the other problems. Statistics roll off our tongues:

- There were 28.5 million adults and children living with HIV and AIDS in Africa by the end of 2001.
- AIDS deaths totalled 3 million globally in 2001, with 2.2 million AIDS deaths occurring in Africa.
- In 1998, 200,000 Africans died in war, but 2 million Africans died of AIDS in the same year.

- In South Africa, 20.1% of adults are infected with HIV.
- With a total of 5 million infected people, South Africa has the world's largest number of people living with HIV/AIDS.[14]

The numbers and tragedy of sickness and death are already such that it is impossible to imagine them, but that is not the end. The psychological trauma of the carers and survivors, the breakdown of family structures, the huge social and financial burden of the orphans left behind, the economic damage and increasing poverty that are caused by the AIDS pandemic cannot be measured.

The world viewed with admiration the outpouring of sympathy and practical assistance that followed the bombing of the World Trade Center in New York on 11 September 2001. Surely there is no comparison with the enormity of the AIDS situation in South Africa. But the proportions of the sympathy and help, both from within and outside the country, are minute compared to the tragedy.

I suggest that the root cause of the disproportionate response of governments and society to the AIDS tragedy is theological – not theology as it is taught in the seminaries and universities, but the theology that is witnessed to by the actions of the Church. In other words, the feeling that AIDS sufferers are somehow guilty and therefore not as worthy of help as, say, the 'innocent' victims in the World Trade Center is perpetuated by the moralistic approach to the AIDS crisis.

A scripture-based theology of the responsibility of the Church in the face of AIDS must take account of the following Christian teachings:

> If one of the brothers or one of the sisters is in need of clothes, and has not enough food to live on, and one of you says to him, 'I wish you well; keep yourself warm and eat plenty', without giving them these bare necessities of life, then what good is that? (James 2.15–16)

---

14 Based on statistics in Liz Clarke's article 'AIDS: A New Helping Hand' in the South African *Sunday Tribune*, 1 December 2002 (World AIDSDay), p. 8.

Do not judge and you will not be judged; because the judgements you give are the judgements you will get, and the standards you use will be the standards used for you. Why do you observe the splinter in your brother's eye and never notice the log in your own? And how dare you say to your brother, 'Let me take the splinter out of your eye' when, look, there is a great log in your own? Hypocrite! . . . (Matthew 7.1–5)

Jesus said, 'The scribes and the Pharisees occupy the chair of Moses. You must therefore do and observe what they tell you; but do not be guided by what they do, since they do not practise what they preach. They tie up heavy burdens and lay them on people's shoulders, but will they lift a finger to move them? No, not they! (Matthew 23.1–5)

As he went along, [Jesus] saw a man who was born blind from birth. His disciples asked him, 'Rabbi, who sinned, this man or his parents, that he should have been born blind?' 'Neither he nor his parents have sinned' Jesus answered, 'he was born blind so that the works of God might be revealed in him . . .' (John 9.1–3)

It was about this time that some people arrived and told him about the Galileans whose blood Pilate had mingled with that of the sacrifices. At this he said to them, 'Do you suppose that these Galileans were worse sinners than any others, that this should happen to them? They were not, I tell you . . . Or those eighteen on whom the tower of Siloam fell, killing them all? Do you suppose they were more guilty than other people living in Jerusalem? They were not, I tell you.' (Luke 13.1–5)

Some relevant questions

Do we recognize that there is still a great tendency for the Christian Church to discuss HIV/AIDS in a context of morality? Surely it is more appropriate that Christ's Church, the 'mystical Body of Christ', the concrete making-present of Christ in our place and our time, reacts, and is seen as reacting, to the scourge of AIDS with compassion, support and love? So the tendency to moralize must be actively rejected.

Even if we can claim that no other non-governmental agency in Southern Africa is doing more for AIDS sufferers, can we say it is sufficient if, for example, there are 15 beds for AIDS sufferers in a jurisdiction that has 1 million HIV-positive people? Should we not recognize that we are in a state of major unprecedented crisis that demands mobilization of all resources and a radical re-prioritization?

Can we say that we have had an effective programme to provide our members with a positive appreciation of responsible sexuality, and a supportive community to help them to live accordingly, and, if not, are we justified in maintaining our 'moral high ground' position?

Is our teaching of sexual morality to our youths and adults sufficiently holistic and real to combat the immense power of the media and the surrounding environment? This cannot be done unless our Christian communities become functional families that are loving, supportive and welcoming to all, and particularly that provide our youth with an attractive alternative environment which will relate to them not only at the intellectual level, but listen to and support them in the turmoil that surrounds them.

Is it true to say that the use of condoms is 'part of the problem' when there is credible evidence that a condom-use campaign has drastically reduced the rate of HIV infection in other African countries? It is claimed that promoting the use of condoms in a particular situation can be interpreted as 'condoning promiscuous sexual activity'. A positive teaching that abstinence is the best option, done in a credible, convincing way, will help those who are capable of being helped, but the use of condoms for those who are not at that stage – for emotional, economic and social reasons – can be left as 'better than nothing' if condoms are not actively condemned as evil.

Do we recognize that we have failed the more vulnerable sector of our membership (not to mention society at large) by simply pronouncing moral directives without demonstrating the credibility of our position in a society of powerful counter-witness?

The Church continues to condemn advocating the use of condoms as a prevention of the spread of AIDS, but, while there is clear logic in saying that we cannot recommend something that will be interpreted as condoning immorality, there are individual bishops and theologians who have decided that being a Christian religious leader requires something different. In an interview entitled 'The Church has AIDS' Bishop Kevin Dowling makes the following statement: 'If we simply proclaim a message that condoms cannot be used under any circumstances, then I believe people will find it difficult to believe that we, as a church, are committed to a compassionate and caring response to those who are suffering, often in appalling living conditions. For me, the condom issue is not simply a matter of chastity but of justice.'[15]

Provision by society of adequate help to those who are HIV-positive and have active AIDS is a 'justice issue'. Provision of the protection of condoms against this deadly disease, imperfect as they are, for those who are vulnerable or likely to further spread the disease – such as those Bishop Dowling points to as living in appalling living conditions – is also 'a justice issue'. A German/English booklet published by the Medical Mission Institute, Wuerzburg, Germany, outlines many other expressions of concern about inflexibility about condoms that have been articulated by church leaders in other countries.[16] The recurring theme of the statements of those leaders is precisely in the same area of 'justice for those who are not able to help themselves'.

Does that mean the Church must abdicate its role in teaching and witnessing to an authentic ethic of human sexuality that is in accordance with humankind's dignity and God's vocation? The answer is clearly 'No'. The situation 'in the field', to which any pastor will testify,[17] dramatically illustrates the failure of

---

15 G. Byamugisha *et al.*, 2002, *Journeys of Faith*, St Albans: TALC, p. 95.

16 M. Kieffer, n.d., *Positions Within the Catholic Church Regarding Infection Protection in Context of HIV/AIDS*, Medical Mission Institute, Wuerzburg.

17 I know of parish priests and those who work with young people in educational institutions in South Africa who say that many Catholic youths openly discuss their sexual activities in such a way that they clearly have no moral concerns about the matter.

the Church in South Africa in conveying to its members, much less to society at large, a sexual morality that is both human and dignified. The tragic history of South Africa up to recently played a major part in this lack, but it does illustrate the need for an orchestrated, authentic, sustained campaign to educate our youths as well as adults to a positive, joyful and disciplined appreciation of the gift of God which sexuality is. That campaign must not be seen as a response to AIDS, but a response to a realization of our failure in the past. In order to avoid the image of being judgemental, our education to sexual morality should be separated from our compassionate response to the AIDS pandemic.

The precise content and methodology of such a programme for the youth in our Church is outside the scope of this discourse. Suffice it to say that the following theological points must be made in a language that will speak to the minds and hearts of our young people:

1 Our sexuality is not an 'attribute' that we should fear and ignore as much as possible, but is a beautiful integral part of the human reality.
2 The human body – sexuality and all – is the culmination of God's creating love, who created us in his own image and likeness.
3 There is more to 'love' – the love which Christ made the cornerstone of his new commandment – than feeling and attraction.
4 The attractions of our bodies and emotions must be integrated into our intellectual convictions and beliefs.
5 The human expressions of each kind of relationship have evident boundaries, the observance of which is in the interests of society at large and in the ultimate interest of the people concerned.
6 The joy of overt genital sexual activity is appropriate only when a permanent total commitment has been made. For Catholics that commitment is found in Christian Marriage.

The Church must also exercise its leadership role in society in general by helping to reclaim the sexual mores of a society that has been ravaged by history:

These mores can be inspired by a vision of being fully human, by a specific religious ethos, or by both. I would argue that African tradition (in conjunction with the Judeo-Christian and the Islamic traditions, the other two predominant religious traditions in Africa) provides people with such a vision and such mores. What is needed is, however, not simply a return to some romanticised concept of an idyllic past, but rather reclaiming dimensions of living in community which have been forgotten or repressed because of economic and social devastation.[18]

The responsibility of the Church is to clearly articulate its sympathy and solidarity with all AIDS victims, to show love and non-judgemental acceptance, and to demonstrate that love by directing a massive practical effort to alleviating their physical and emotional sufferings.

I further suggest that if the Church leadership finds itself unable to accept that the use of condoms is appropriate in the context of the South African crisis, the acceptable Christian position would be to refrain from condemning those who see condoms as one of the few methods available at present to contain the epidemic. 'Turning a blind eye' might seem to be a cowardly posture to adopt, but there is precedent in church history for such a policy being considered moral.[19] Basil of Caesarea lived in the turmoil of the Trinitarian heresies of the fifth century. At a time when the articulation of a particular belief about, say, the divinity and humanity of Christ could plunge a whole nation into civil war resulting in thousands of deaths, he adopted a policy that is called '*Oikonomia*' – an economy of words.

Basil believed explicitly in the divinity of the Holy Spirit. He was surrounded by bishops and other leaders who denied that divinity. Insisting on that belief would lead to civil turmoil, so

---

18 W. Saayman, 1994, 'AIDS' in Charles Villa-Vicencio and John W. de Gruchy (eds), *Doing Ethics in Context – South African Perspectives*, Capetown: David Philip/Orbis, p. 176.

19 See C. P. Ryan, 1997, *Basil and Controversy: A Moral Appraisal*, Rome: Academia Alfonsiana.

he decided to live and die without ever stating explicitly that 'the Holy Spirit is God'. He knew that the truth would eventually emerge but he made a prudential judgement that his time and place was not the setting for insisting on it. We know that distributing condoms is not the best way of solving our present major problems, but let us not condemn until the better solution is actually in place.

The prophetic role of the Catholic Church in Southern Africa cannot be set aside. We must continue to use all possible means to cry out against injustice in all its forms in our society. The Church has the moral leadership to motivate government and public bodies to allocate a higher and higher proportion of resources to research, suffering alleviation, appropriate education and use of the media in the face of the present ongoing tragedy.

But in dealing with the vast number of people and communities that are being ravaged by a disease that no one could deserve, the compassionate, healing and forgiving face of Christ must be clearly seen.

5. The Church, Homosexuality and AIDS

GARETH MOORE

There are a number of ways in which HIV, the virus responsible for AIDS, is transmitted, but still by far the most important worldwide and in particular in the West is sexual transmission. In America and Europe a major and growing route of infection is needle sharing among drug abusers, but it has spread mainly, though far from exclusively, through homosexual contact between men. [Editor's note: this was written in 1990.] It is this sexual aspect of AIDS, and its connection with homosexuality, that has made it so controversial, and which has made it so problematic for the Church to find a proper response to it. So it is on AIDS, sex and the Church that I shall focus.

What is the proper attitude of the Church to AIDS? One thing to be said first of all is that the Church's ministry is one of word and deed. As a body we seek both to proclaim the gospel and to bring ordinary human comfort to those in need, whoever they may be. We not only preach, teach and defend a message; we also tend the sick, feed the hungry, visit those in prison, and so on. We lay before people the possibility of a fuller life and help them to share in the life that we ourselves have received. The two belong together; ours is a practical gospel. We cannot, as Church, preach the commandments of Christ without being committed to obeying them; we cannot preach his love for us and for all without letting that love reach others through us. In the particular case of AIDS it is up to us to speak and to act in ways that communicate the gospel, that bring life and comfort. This will include on the one hand teaching people how they can avoid contracting HIV and on the other caring for those who have contracted HIV and may have gone on to develop AIDS, as well as caring for their families, friends and lovers.

There can be no doubt that, despite some initial hesitation in the face of the unknown, the Church is and will be willing to care as best it can for the physical and spiritual needs of those with AIDS and HIV infection. The physical care of the sick and dying has always been an important part of the Church's task, as has the bringing of comfort and the assurance of the love of God to the distressed and those faced with imminent death. AIDS is no exception, and laity and clergy alike, as individuals and in groups, are already doing much work in this area, bringing comfort to those sick at home or in hospital, or giving education, advice and practical help through AIDS-related charities.

But there is a problem in giving full rein to this willingness. The problem is at the level of what the Church says, of teaching and moral theology and of traditional attitudes in the Church to sex in general and to homosexuality in particular. It appears to me that in a number of ways the Church has been and still is in danger of failing in its mission, failing to contribute what it can to the problem of AIDS.

First, and this is a relatively minor shortcoming, there has been a certain amount of what might be called theological opportunism, a tendency to make theological capital out of people's suffering. There have been those who have tried to conscript AIDS into the service of some particular theological or moral viewpoint. Some have gone so far as to call AIDS divine punishment on perverts, or in general a judgement from heaven on the corruption of earth. Thankfully, less has been heard of late from the wrath-of-God brigade, but more subtle variations on the same theme continue to be sounded: AIDS is a warning that there is a sickness in Western society, or a reminder from God that the proper place of sex is in marriage, a divine vindication of Catholic or Christian teaching. But there is little purpose to be served by making these claims; they sound too much either like Christians scoring points off unbelievers or like Christian self-flagellation, and do little to help the Church evolve a practical response. And they are in any case inherently implausible. There is no reason why we should see AIDS as a sign from God of the moral degeneracy of our times. Nor is it a divine warning in particular against deviant or unchristian sexual practices. We should not forget that there has always been a fair amount of moral degeneracy, and there have always been deviant sexual practices; and most of this has gone on in safety, without catastrophic consequences for those involved. What has caused this tragedy for so many people is not their depravity but a novel and deadly virus, which we hope to be able to deal with before too long. (And even in the age of HIV, much deviant sex still goes on without fatal consequences; the spread of safer sex information has been a help here.) The idea that God might use such a deadly but blunt instrument as AIDS to convey his message, as well as being repulsive, is not consonant with what we know of him from Christ. What God wants to convey to us, he does so not through catastrophe but through the gospel.

It has been said, too, that a possible divine purpose of AIDS, and one possible beneficial result of it, is to lead people to a rediscovery of chastity. But there is no reason to believe this, either. One thing that AIDS has certainly done in the West is to make many people rethink their sexual attitudes and re-form their sexual lifestyle, and in a direction the Church must approve of. But this is far from saying that AIDS has made people rediscover the Christian virtue of chastity. Chastity as understood by Christians is, after all, not merely a matter of sexual abstinence for the unmarried: it involves an orientation of oneself towards God and valuing of human relationships and of one's sexual faculties as gifts of God. The current AIDS scare may have brought this about in a few cases, though it is not easy to see how. It can be said that on the whole AIDS does not teach people chastity; it only teaches them fear. It may be that in some cases fear has a certain shock value. The realization that they are exposing themselves or their friends to danger of death, or the illness and death of those around them, may bring some people to see the emptiness of a way of life based on sex. But we cannot see this as a good side of AIDS. There are better, less painful, more human ways of learning this lesson. And there is no reason anyway to believe that this is the lesson that is learnt in most cases. Most people have reacted not with chastity but with condoms. What they have learnt is only that it is necessary to be cautious for a while, until a successful treatment is found.

That there will eventually be a successful treatment is something to be prayed for and expected. Already considerable advances have been made, and from the amount of research that is going on it seems likely that it will not be many years before AIDS can be cured, or at least made survivable. And until then it can be avoided by safer sex practices which are, for those in danger of contracting or transmitting HIV infection, much more convenient and attractive than the complete abstinence the Church recommends to them as part of the ordering of their life towards God. In such circumstances it is simply mistaken to say that the Church is the key to beating AIDS, that AIDS can only be eliminated by everybody living as the Church would have them live. The Church's teaching on sex may have many things to recommend it, but its effectiveness for preventing AIDS is not one of them.

But if some theological theorizing about AIDS is unhelpful, it nevertheless remains true that, in a certain sense, the Church, in its teaching on sex and marriage, *does* have a key to the elimination of AIDS, if only people would follow it. For HIV infection is spread from person to person by means of infected body fluids; and though it can be transmitted in a number of ways – by using infected needles, or from mother to child in the womb or through breast milk – it is mostly through intimate sexual contact that people get HIV into their system. Mostly, you get HIV by having sex with an infected person in such a way that their bodily fluids can enter your body.

Part of the Church's teaching on sex is that genital activity belongs within the bounds of marriage. The Church did not come to this teaching because it makes for hygienic sex. It reflects the belief that sex is ordered by God for the generation of children and for the expression of a love open to embrace children, and that the divinely ordained institution of marriage is the proper setting for such love and for the care of children. Its basis is theological rather than medicinal. Nevertheless, in the context of AIDS the Church's teaching has obvious benefits. If everybody had followed it, AIDS would have spread much less than it in fact has, if at all. And if everybody now followed the Church's teaching on sex, the spread of AIDS would be greatly slowed and the syndrome could eventually be eliminated. It can be argued that by sticking steadfastly to its teaching, the Church is performing an important service. If the Church can get people to listen to its teaching and to follow it, if it can persuade the unmarried to remain genitally inactive and the married to confine their genital activity to their marriage partner, it will be protecting them from HIV infection and from possible death from AIDS.

So much is obvious. But it is equally obvious that the Church will not succeed in this. At any rate, it will not succeed quickly enough to be of significant help in combating AIDS. Not only are there many places where the Church's voice is not heard, but even where it is heard its teaching is not heeded. This is partly because of simple individual sinfulness, because people cannot face up to the strains of following a teaching they know to be right. But for many people, Catholics included, things are not so simple. Many people, Catholics included, find the Church's teaching not only uncongenial or difficult, but also unconvincing or even straightforwardly wrong. And they may hold this view not because they refuse to listen to what the Church has to say, but because, having listened, they have found the Church's doctrine wanting; in other words, they hold this view not because they won't think, but as a result of their thinking. They may think it perfectly legitimate to have sexual relations outside marriage, perhaps with more than one partner, perhaps with a partner or partners of the same sex.

What is the Church to do in this situation? The first thing to recognize is that the Church itself must take part of the responsibility if its voice is not heard. The Church already has a bad reputation, both within and without, for its human insensitivity in matters sexual. This reputation is not entirely undeserved. Part of the problem lies with the content of the Church's teaching. It proclaims a lofty sexual ideal, but the predictable effect of this is to make many within the Church feel guilty and to see their sexuality as something essentially problematic. This includes not only those Catholics who fail to live up to the Church's ideal, but also those who cannot even bring themselves to share that ideal. There are the 'weak', those who basically accept the Church's teaching but find themselves all too often defeated by the strength of the temptations they face. But there is also another group: those to whom the lofty ideal of the Church simply does not speak; those who, like many Catholic homosexuals, cannot subscribe to the Church's official doctrine because their sexuality leads them in a different direction, who cannot in all conscience understand why their sexual desires are regarded in the Church as pathological, their sexual activity as sinful and unacceptable. This second group have a deeper difficulty than the first. Not only are they encouraged to see themselves as sinful by virtue of their sexuality, but they are also encouraged to doubt whether, since they are at odds with the Church in such an important area of life, and an area which the Church constantly brings to their attention, they have any genuine place in the Church at all. Many such people end up leaving the Church, sometimes painfully. Those who stay often do so only uneasily, and they can do little more than maintain a guilty and bewildered silence.

If difficulties are caused by the content of what the Church teaches in this area, they arise too from the style and tone of that teaching. Too often the Church speaks the language of strident condemnation when it comes across behaviour it does not approve of, especially sexual behaviour. The tone of the Ratzinger *Letter on the Pastoral Care of Homosexual Persons* is a recent case in point. An obvious remark to be made about such language is that, while it might please the right-thinking and confirm them in their views, it alienates those at whom it is primarily directed, those who for one reason or another do not follow the Church's teaching. Though the *Letter* does in its later paragraphs go on to speak of the Church's concern for homosexuals, the average homosexual – and particularly the average Catholic homosexual – can be forgiven for not being terribly convinced; he or she will not be filled with enthusiasm at the idea of rushing into the consoling arms of compassionate, caring Mother Church. And in fact it has been the experience of many homosexuals that Mother Church, as represented by her ministers as well as laity, is often far from compassionate and consoling: too often it is only condemnation that they receive.

There are Catholic organizations designed to give support to homosexuals, such as Quest in the United Kingdom and Dignity in the United States. These certainly do what they can to make homosexuals feel they have a place in the Church and to give them an opportunity to speak freely and be listened to. But there are many whom these associations do not reach; many do not know they exist, and it can require a certain courage even to join one. Since the Ratzinger *Letter*, life has become more difficult for some of them. For most homosexuals in the Church, the only regular forum they have for discussing their sexuality and their sexual practices is the normally guilt-ridden session in the confessional. Here, though there are sensitive and sympathetic priests, the experience is too often anything but helpful, and the penitent, especially the sexually deviant, experiences only condemnation or an uneasy silence from the other side of the grille.

Thus those whom the Church professes to love it often succeeds only in burdening and alienating. Nobody in such a position is liable to see the Church as a possible helper, a place where he or she can turn in time of need. Still less are such people *encouraged* to seek help from the Church. In effect, the Church ends up denying itself as a source of strength and comfort for those who need it as much as anybody else does, and sometimes more. To the extent to which the Church thus makes itself unavailable to help people, it is failing in its God-given mission to relieve suffering, and may even stand accused of itself causing suffering.

This, regrettable in itself, is an even more serious matter in the age of AIDS, because, in the West, it is still mostly homosexual men – one of the groups who find themselves most alienated from the Church – who contract HIV and suffer from AIDS. Homosexual men with HIV or AIDS often need material and spiritual help. The Church may be there, ready to help, as it is always ready to help the sick and dying. But how many will actually *want* the Church's help? Put simply, if you were a homosexual man and had just discovered you were HIV-positive, would the first person you went to tell be your parish priest? For many, he would be the last.

These people whom the Church alienates are clearly in more danger of contracting HIV than those who practise what the

Church preaches, and this is especially true of those who do not limit their sexual activity to one partner. There is also more danger of them transmitting it to others. This is an important matter for the Church, which is concerned whenever human life is threatened. What can the Church do about it? It is not enough to say that the Church must go on preaching its own chaste vision of sex when we know that there are those who do not share it and are sincerely convinced it is wrong, and when we know that there are those who, though they may be convinced Catholics, are simply weak-willed when it comes to sex. We cannot at this point say that if somebody is determined not to follow the Church's way, 'determined to sin', then the consequences are his or her own responsibility. We cannot be content that the Catholic has done his or her job in presenting the Christian vision of life; that if the people concerned reject it, as they are free to do, then there is no more that we can or should do. It is not enough for the Church to wait, ready to show them compassion if and when they come down with AIDS. It is not enough to say that they are at the heart of the Church when they get AIDS, if they have effectively been banished to the margins, alienated and then ignored before they get AIDS. To adopt this attitude is also to neglect our responsibility to any others who may be endangered by their behaviour; it is to abdicate the obvious Christian responsibility to help preserve life. This route is simply not open to Christians.

What the Church says and what it does in pastoral practice inevitably hang together. Those who are actively engaged in the Church's caring ministry need not at the same time be moral theologians, and they may not be in a position to keep up to date with pastoral guidelines issued by the teaching authorities of the Church nationally or internationally. But pastoral care cannot simply go its own way. Pastoral practice which deliberately ignores the Church's moral teaching is in danger of being in bad faith. It can also produce confusion on the part of those who are supposed to be helped. No responsible Catholic pastoral worker wants to allow this to happen. But on the other hand, effective pastoral work is a prime part of the Church's responsibility. This means that what the Church says in the moral sphere must facilitate pastoral practice. It is not open to us to say that the Church teaches the truth and that it is unfortunate if the truth has disastrous pastoral consequences. A theological approach that makes effective pastoral care more difficult needs to be changed. And it is not only the pastoral side that suffers. A further point is that by its approach the Church invites failure also in its teaching and preaching mission. For the Church's duty is not simply to speak, but to speak so that others might hear. The alienated do not listen, and cannot reasonably be expected to listen.

By what it teaches and the tone in which it often speaks in public and in private, the Church cuts itself off from being a resource for people suffering from AIDS or HIV infection. Christ commanded his followers to visit the sick. He made no exception, and neither does the Church make any exception, of the homosexual sick, not even of the promiscuous homosexual sick. But if our visits are to be welcomed, then, at the very least, a new tone has to be found.

If there is a problem for those who need help, there is also one for many who would give it. When a priest is unhelpful it is not always because he is lacking in human sympathy and under-standing. It can be because he is striving to be faithful to what the Church teaches. He is caught in a bind because any gesture of sympathy on his part can seem like condoning sin, or as a betrayal of the Church whose servant he is. Similar problems can arise for those many Catholics who either do work or want to work alongside others to combat the spread of AIDS – in the medical professions, or as members of voluntary organizations. Often such work involves giving advice on safer sex practices, practices which may well be, according to the teaching of the Church, sinful. An obvious question is, can Catholics do this and remain faithful to the Church? For instance, can a Catholic give advice, with a clear conscience, to homosexual men on safer sex? However worthy the cause, however desirable it may be to stop the spread of the disease, is this not to condone, even actively to encourage, sin? The Catholic should by all means urge the homosexual to live in accordance with church teach-ing, that is to give up all his sexual activity, to stop sinning. But if his advice is not heeded or is openly rejected – and it is very probable that that is what is going to happen – it seems he can do little more. For is not giving such advice and information a matter of telling people how to sin safely? Surely no Catholic can get involved in this sort of thing. In traditional Catholic theology it is never permissible to do moral evil, to sin, that good may come. However good the end may be, if the only means a Christian has of helping to stop the spread of the disease is to sin by encouraging others to commit sin, then he or she may not do so.

Is it possible to say anything useful here without abandoning traditional teaching on sex? There are many who would argue that such teaching should be abandoned or at least modified. But it is unnecessary to get into that argument when we are concerned with AIDS. In fact, even from the most traditional standpoint, it is not necessary to encourage sin to save lives. It is possible for a Catholic to give, in good conscience, the advice that might be essential to saving life, however much the Church may disapprove of particular sexual practices. It has traditionally and rightly been held in Catholic moral theology that you should not sin at all, but that if you are resolved to perform a sinful action it is still incumbent on you to minimize the evil that your action involves. You may, despite all advice or entreaty to the contrary, be resolved to commit murder, which is an evil. But your moral responsibility does not end with your decision to commit an evil act. It is still up to you to sin in the way that causes least evil, not to kill by a method that causes your victim unnecessary suffering, not to kill indiscriminately in order to get at your target, say, by blowing up a bus or a plane; and so on. This same principle applies here. If, for example, a man is resolved, perhaps in good conscience, to continue in a sexual relationship with his male lover, and if we, in line with the Vatican and traditional teaching, regard that as an objective moral evil, it is still up to him to minimize the evil of his act. If he is going to continue his relationship (in which there may be much good), it is important that as little evil as possible should result from its sexual side. That is, it is morally important that he should not act in such a way as, among other things, to contribute to the spread of AIDS. He should, for example, be sure to remain faithful to his partner. If there is danger that one of them be already infected, he should perform those kinds of sex acts with his partner that minimize the chance of HIV passing between them. Since any Catholic can be concerned to minimize the evil consequences of other people's behaviour, it is perfectly in order to give advice on how this can be done, or give information on how such advice can be obtained. It is also good to encourage the stability of the relationship and sexual fidelity within it. This is not to encourage homosexual relationships; it is only to say that *if* people form such relationships *then* it is better that they be stable.

The point can be put another way. It is possible to speak of a fully human life lived in accordance with the virtues. Homosexual practices, like all sex outside marriage, have traditionally been seen as a way of failing specifically to live out the virtue of chastity. With the advent of AIDS the moral picture has changed somewhat. At a time when sex can be fatal, the Church cannot speak about it simply in terms of chastity. The man or woman who has multiple sex partners and exchanges body fluids with them multiplies his or her chances both of picking up HIV and of infecting others. The risk can be much reduced if precautions are taken. To fail to take those precautions is to show extreme lack of concern for one's sexual partners. It is to lack charity. For to put the life of somebody else in danger is to sin against the virtue of charity, which involves, among other things, cherishing the life of others. It is also to show a lack of proper concern for oneself. It is to sin against the virtue of prudence, which involves, in ordinary circumstances, taking sensible precautions to preserve one's own life and health. It is not possible now, if it ever was, to regard chastity as the only consideration in sex. Now, what people do sexually is not just a matter of how far they keep themselves pure and live up to an exalted ideal, but of the most elementary love for others and for themselves.

If somebody is resolved to act in a way that the Church regards as unchaste, it is still his responsibility as a moral agent not to act uncharitably or imprudently. If modifying his sexual behaviour in certain ways reduces the risk of catching or of passing on HIV, to do so would be an exercise of charity and of prudence, so even if he will not abandon his sexual activity altogether he should modify it. Indeed, most people, Catholic or not, if they become properly aware of the dangers involved in what they are doing, will want to modify their behaviour.

Anybody who helps people to do that, for instance by giving advice on safer sex, is assisting in the exercise of virtue. To give advice on safer sex is not to give advice on safer sin, and in no way involves condoning or approving any activity condemned by the Church as unchaste and therefore sinful. It is, on the contrary, an attempt to prevent sin, and as such is something that any Catholic can do with a clear conscience, part of the work of the Church. Indeed, to refuse to give such advice, should the opportunity present itself, might well be regarded as sinful, since it is shirking the Church's mission to protect life and promote virtue, to preserve bodies and nourish souls.

6. Jesus, Prophecy and AIDS

MUSA W. DUBE

All Synoptic Gospels attest that when Jesus was baptized, the Spirit came upon him (Mark 1.9–11; Luke 3.21–22; Matthew 3.13–17). According to the Gospel of Luke, when Jesus returned from the wilderness, where he was tempted,

> He came to Nazareth, where he had been brought up, he went to the synagogue on the sabbath day, as was his custom. He stood up to read, and the scroll of the prophet Isaiah was given to him. He unrolled the scroll and found the place where it was written: 'The Spirit of the Lord is upon me, because he has anointed me to bring good news to the poor. He has sent me to proclaim release to the captives and recovery of sight to the blind, to let the oppressed go free, to proclaim the year of the Lord's favour.' (Luke 4.16–19)

The story goes on to say that Jesus

> rolled up the scroll, gave it back to the attendant, and sat down. The eyes of all in the synagogue were fixed on him. Then he began to say to them, 'Today this scripture has been fulfilled in your hearing.' All spoke well of him and were amazed at the gracious words that came from his mouth. They said, 'Is not this Joseph's son?' (Luke 4.20–22)

Jesus not only read from the words and book of Isaiah the prophet, he also identified himself with this prophet and took up his prophetic agenda. This is clear in the words he added after he finished his reading, namely, 'today this scripture has been fulfilled in your hearing' (v. 21). Further, the content of his chosen passage is prophetic since it highlights that Jesus dedicated his ministry to challenging social injustice by pronouncing liberation to the poor, the captives and the sick. Jesus also announced hope since he came 'to proclaim the year of the Lord's favour'. That is, he came to proclaim the Jubilee or social and economic justice for all members of the society (Leviticus 25.8–55). This, in my reading, is the gospel, and speaks justice and wellness in all aspects of our lives.

The significance of this passage, as many scholars have pointed out, lies in the fact that, according to Luke, Jesus used it to unveil the agenda of his public ministry. This agenda is highlighted as a prophetic role of speaking hope to the hopeless, and calling for justice for those whose rights are trampled upon. But, and perhaps most importantly, the significance of the passage lies in the willingness of Jesus to take up the prophetic role – to announce simply and courageously that 'the Spirit of the Lord is upon me!' It is the Spirit of the Lord which, when it is upon us, brings the word of the Lord upon us and enables us to speak the good news to God's people. His listeners, who responded first with silence, grasped Jesus' assumption of this prophetic role and 'all eyes were fixed on him'. When Jesus interpreted the passage to them, saying, 'today this scripture is fulfilled in your midst', then they were glad, and said, 'Is this not Joseph's son?' In other words, the audience was saying, is this not the boy from our neighbourhood? Is this not the child whose parents are known to us? Remember, Jesus had come to Nazareth, his home place where everyone knew him. And so they ask, 'Does the Spirit of the Lord come upon such ordinary people in our neighbourhood?' Should prophets rise and speak in our home towns? Yes, the text tells us.

Apart from his own self-identification with prophets, the people around Jesus also identified him with prophets. We learn that when Herod heard about the deeds of Jesus, he suspected that John the Baptist had been raised from death (Mark 6; Luke 9.7–9); some identified him with Elijah (Luke 9.8). But perhaps the most significant indication that Jesus was generally identified with prophets is the passage where Jesus paused to do an evaluation of his ministry by asking his disciples, 'Who do people say that the Son of Man is?' And they said, 'Some say John the Baptist, but others Elijah, and still others Jeremiah or one of the prophets' (Matthew 16.13–14). The general perception was that Jesus was a prophet, as he was firmly identified with them. Jesus did not deny this identification with prophets. In fact, the Gospel of Luke, which holds that he began by identifying himself with prophets, also affirms that as he went towards the end of his public ministry, when he knowingly travelled to Jerusalem to meet his death, he said, 'It is impossible for a prophet to be killed outside of Jerusalem' (13.33). The prophetic role of Jesus was attested by his concern for social justice.

Social justice: 'God will quickly grant justice to them'

Jesus' prophetic role is also attested to by the fact that he sided with the least privileged members of his society. He was found together with prostitutes and tax collectors (Luke 18.9–14, 19.1–10) and he took the part of widows (Luke 7.11–17, 21.1–3). He took sides, too, with children and the sick. Jesus' association with despised groups raised eyebrows among other holy teachers. But Jesus did not hesitate to look his fellow teachers in the eye and say to them, 'Tax collectors and prostitutes are going into the kingdom of God ahead of you' (Matthew 21.31). Talking of a widow whose needs were neglected by a powerful judge, Jesus asked, 'And will not God grant justice to chosen ones who cry to God day and night? Will God delay long in helping them? I tell you, God will quickly grant justice to them' (Luke 18.7–8). I believe this last sentence should inform our perspective towards social injustice; that is, God's desire is that justice must be quickly granted to the marginalized.

Second, all the Gospels attest strongly to the fact that Jesus healed people who were sick with many different diseases (Mark 1.29–45). Not only did he heal them from physical illness, he healed them from social and psychological illness also. This is evident when he touched and healed the dreaded lepers, thus restoring them to both physical and social health. Lepers were isolated from the rest of the society. By touching them,

Jesus broke the stigma, the fear that surrounded their illness. By healing them, he restored them back to the society. Jesus also dealt with psychological illnesses engendered by social oppression; there are many stories of him exorcizing evil spirits that had taken possession of people, denying them normal life (Matthew 15.21–28; Luke 8.26–39). Sometimes he preferred to forgive people their sins (Luke 7.47–48), thus restoring their spiritual health. In short, Jesus sought the total health of people, thus demonstrating that it is God's will that all should be fully healed economically, socially and physically. Certainly Jesus' holistic healing ministry offers us a firm theological framework, a basis upon which we should insist on healing as a divine right for all people.

Even in Jesus' day, and among his people, there were those who were discriminated against on the basis of their race. Good examples were the Samaritans and Canaanites. The ministry of Jesus made efforts to break racial and ethnic stigma. When Jesus asked for water from a Samaritan woman, she was surprised and said, 'How is it that you, a Jew, ask a drink of me, a woman of Samaria?' (John 4.9). The narrator explains to us, 'Jews do not share things in common with Samaritans.' The parable of the Good Samaritan is another good example. Here Jesus showed that a Jewish priest and a Levite are not necessarily better than a Samaritan (Luke 10.25–37), and that, in fact, a Samaritan has better social values. This point is also underlined in the story of ten lepers who were healed (Luke 17.11–19). But Jesus also had to confront his own racial and ethnic discrimination. This is evident in the story of the Canaanite woman, who came to ask him to heal her daughter possessed by a demon (Matthew 15.21–28). Jesus did not talk to her and did not wish to help her, for he held that he was sent only to the lost sheep of Israel. When the woman finally fell before him, begging for his mercy, Jesus did not hesitate to tell her that he could not take the children's food and throw it to the dogs (v. 26). But this face-to-face confrontation with a Canaanite woman, who also pointed out in her own way that Canaanite children are also children who need the bread of healing, brought Jesus to revise his stand.

Jesus' association with the less privileged is also evident in his relationship with women. Women of his time and society, as in most of our societies, were denied economic, decision-making, leadership and legal power on the basis of their gender. Jesus began to fight for gender justice by befriending women (John 11), allowing them to follow him (Luke 8.1–3), allowing the unclean bleeding woman to touch him (Mark 5.24–34), sending them to preach (John 4.39–42, 20.17), thus giving them public leadership roles. He also insisted that the law should apply to and protect both women and men (John 8.1–11). At one point we hear that his own disciples were surprised to find him talking to a woman by the well. The story tells us, however, that none of them dared to say, 'What do you want?' or 'Why are you speaking with her?' (John 4.27). I think this is an important point – that even though during Jesus' time there were gender divisions, he brought his disciples to realize and to accept that he talked to women! Jesus revealed himself to them, causing them to leave behind their water containers (John 4.28).

Religious hypocrisy: 'You have neglected weightier matters'

Jesus' prophetic role is also evident in the fact that he challenged faith practices tolerant of social injustice. This is attested by his approach to ancient scriptures and their interpretation, as well as his attitude towards the religious and national leaders of his day.

To start with the scriptures, Jesus made it clear that they are holy and will not change, but they should never be used to endorse social oppression. This comes through in his Sermon on the Mount and the numerous debates he had with Pharisees regarding the sabbath. In Matthew 5.17–18, he began by asserting that not one iota would be removed from the scriptures, for he had come to fulfil them. After this, he began to quote the scriptures and change them. This was done in formulaic style, which began, 'You have heard that it was said to those of ancient times . . .', then he quoted from the scriptures. He went on to say, 'But I say to you . . .' In this second part, Jesus reformulated what was said by the ancient scriptures (5.17–47).

One good example is, 'You have heard that it was said to those of ancient times, "You shall not swear falsely, but carry out the vows you have made to the Lord." But I say to you, Do not swear at all . . . Let your word be "Yes, Yes" or "No, No"' (vv. 33–34, 37). Scholars have argued about what Jesus was doing: was he changing the scriptures or just interpreting them? I think he did both. What I regard as important is that Jesus would not tolerate any injustice that is legitimized by saying, 'It is written in the scriptures.' Rather, he had the courage to say prophetically, 'But I say to you.' He was ready to say that if what is written has come to support corruption, injustice and oppression, then it must go, for the word of the Lord must affirm God's people, not oppress them.

This standpoint is further attested in his debates with his fellow Jewish teachers on the subject of what could or could not be done during the sabbath. Jesus healed on the sabbath (Luke 6.1–11, 13.10–17, 14.1–6); harvested fruits to eat, and when his fellow teachers protested, he said to them, 'I ask you, is it lawful to do good or to do harm on the sabbath, to save life or to destroy it?' (Luke 6.9). Jesus was insistent that, although it is in the law that we must keep the sabbath, we must not lose sight of the fact that 'the sabbath was made for humankind, and not humankind for the sabbath' (Mark 2.27).

Not only did Jesus feel free to challenge as ungodly the scriptures that were used to further injustice, he also challenged religious leaders who upheld such interpretations. We have already said that Jesus was always debating with the Pharisees over the sabbath. Generally, he criticized their whole approach to religion, as in Matthew 23 where he begins by acknowledging their power and their teaching but faults their practice (vv. 1–3). These religious leaders, Jesus held, 'tie up heavy burdens, hard to bear, and lay them on the shoulders of others; but they themselves are unwilling to lift a finger to move them' (v. 4). They 'lock people out of the kingdom of heaven' (vv. 13–14). Jesus made scathing criticism of Pharisees and scribes for their religious hypocrisy. Echoing both Amos and Hosea, he told them the problem is that they 'tithe mint, dill and cumin', and yet they had 'neglected the weightier matters of the law: justice and mercy and faith' (23.23). Although Jesus was in less direct confrontation with the Sadducees, he was not afraid to tell them where their religiosity was hypocritical and unacceptable because it authorized social injustice.

King Herod was frightened: 'The king of the Jews is born'

Lastly, Jesus' prophetic role also targeted oppressive international relations. Jesus was born, lived and died in a colonized state. The Jews, though a people of God, were ruled by the Roman Empire, which stationed its agents, such as Pontius Pilate, King Herod, centurions and soldiers, in the state to prevent revolt. That Jesus was subversive to colonial rule is attested at his birth, when King Herod and his Jerusalem collaborators were disturbed by the announcement that a king had been born to the Jews (Matthew 2.1–15). This Christmas story that we enact annually was politically loaded, for Jesus is characterized as a Moses, one who will be called out of Egypt to liberate God's people (v. 15).

Jesus also preached a subversive message when he announced that the Kingdom of God is near, indeed that it is already here! If the Kingdom of God is here, then Pilate, Herod and their national collaborators do well to tremble, for their days are numbered. With the announcement of another Kingdom, their authority is declared oppressive and unacceptable before God. The announcement was a prophetic challenge to oppressive international and national political structures.

The prophetic message of Jesus and HIV/AIDS

There are many other characteristics that could be highlighted to indicate the prophetic role of Jesus, such as his attitude to wealth. How can recapturing the prophetic message of Jesus help us in fighting HIV/AIDS? It should help to know that Jesus:

- was a prophet who condemned social injustice;
- took sides with the marginalized members of the society such as tax collectors, widows, sex workers, children and lepers;

95

- healed all forms of sickness, without asking how the person got the illness, thus underlining that health is God's will for all of us;
- not only healed lepers, who were feared and isolated, but also touched them and restored them back to society: this should help us to confront the stigma of HIV/AIDS and to minister to the sick;
- empowered women and children: *Facing AIDS: The Challenge, the Churches' Response*, the WCC study document, writes that 'whenever gender discrimination leaves women under-educated, underskilled and unable to gain a title to property or other vital resources, it also makes them vulnerable to HIV/AIDS infection'.[1] It should, therefore, help us in the struggle against HIV/AIDS to know that Jesus began gender empowerment by allowing women to make their own decisions (John 4.28–29) and giving them public leadership roles (John 20.17–18). HIV/AIDS research indicates that the epidemic is fuelled by gender inequalities in our societies. The Christian Church should highlight the gospel of Christ, showing that gender inequality is unchristian;
- forgave sins or what was held to be immoral lifestyles: if the Church is often caught in the trap of condemning those who are infected, saying they are reaping the fruits of their acts, if the Church is so convinced that these people have sinned, it should help Christians to know that Jesus forgave sins. Why should the Church count and recount anybody's sins, if Jesus (the founder and Lord of the Church) forgave them?
- questioned oppressive scriptures: if there are any scriptures used by church leaders and other believers to perpetuate the oppression of God's people, we are free to ask them, 'Is it lawful to save life or to destroy it?' We can say to them, 'It is written, but I say to you . . . ' Yes, even if we are ordinary daughters and sons of Joseph, we are empowered to say, 'The Spirit of the Lord is upon me.' Let me push this point further to its logical end: can we say, echoing Mark 2.27, that the Bible was made for people, not people for the Bible?

---

1 World Council of Churches, 1997, *Facing AIDS: The Challenge, the Churches' Response*, p. 16.

- openly contested oppressive leaders: if our religious leaders and institutions are giving us policies and traditions that hinder our fight against HIV/AIDS, we should be free to criticize these policies as oppressive and ungodly. Are we free to act independently, according to the gospel of Christ?
- was not afraid of the imperial rulers of his time: similarly, we should be prophetic about international relations that perpetrate poverty, such as globalization and heavy debts, which make it difficult for many developing-world governments to struggle effectively against HIV/AIDS. We should be critical of those who are making access to HIV/AIDS drugs difficult. For we have the mandate to insist that the earth and everything in it belongs to the Lord, and that all members of humanity were made in God's image and given the right of access to God's material resources (Genesis 1.26–31).

A prophetic Church: 'I will pour my Spirit upon all flesh'

Some may be thinking, 'Well, yes, but we are not prophets. We are not called. The Spirit of the Lord is not upon us!' I am sure we cannot say this, because of the following New Testament affirmations:

1 Upon his death and resurrection, Jesus commissioned the believers to go and teach what he taught (Matthew 28.18–20). If we are persuaded that Jesus was a prophet, then Christ's followers must also be prophetic. Those who train Christian and church leaders must teach them to be prophetic leaders, who foster prophetic congregations and faith communities. Yet perhaps what we need here is to understand fully what Jesus Christ taught. As we have seen, his teachings and deeds included preaching the good news to the poor, healing the sick, breaking social stigmas, criticizing oppressive institutions and scriptures in order to empower women, children, Samaritans and other marginalized groups. This constituted the gospel of Christ.

2 At the very founding of the Church, the Spirit of the Lord

was poured 'upon all flesh' of the believers, giving Christians the power to speak (Acts 2.1–22). They all began to speak in tongues. On the basis of the fact that the Spirit of the Lord has been poured upon all of us, then we can all confidently go back to our cities, towns, villages, places of residence or work, and simply say, 'The Spirit of the Lord is upon me, because he has anointed me to bring good news to the poor. He has sent me to proclaim release to the captives and recovery of sight to the blind, to let the oppressed go free, to proclaim the year of the Lord's favour' (Luke 4.18–19).

3 If we do not prophesy, then we are not living out our Christian faith, for we have all been called and sent to go out and call. If we do not prophesy, we are failing Jesus Christ who sent the Church to speak and gave the Church the Spirit to prophesy. And in this HIV/AIDS epidemic, whom shall the Lord send but us? But of course, as Palma tells us,[2] it is instructive to realize that prophecy involves willingness on our side: to be open to the Spirit – the Spirit that enables us to discern and denounce injustice as well as to speak hope and justice to God's people. The option to be the prophet Jonah is there, and sometimes God does not want or need to bury us in the stomach of a whale in order to bring us back to our responsibility.

Teaching our student ministers to prophesy

Some may ask, if prophets are called and sent by God, how we can teach our student trainee ministers to be prophets – this is out of our hands. This model is shown us in the Bible. There were Elijah and Elisha (2 Kings 2.3, 4.38, 6.1–2), there was John the Baptist and his disciples, and Jesus Christ had disciples. Disciples are students, those who are learning from their teacher. The Gospels attest that Jesus sometimes sent his disci-

---

2 Marta Palma and Marianne Bickerstaff Mosian, 1996, 'Prophecy, Women's Church' and 'Prophets and Biblical Women' in Letty Russell and J. Shannon Clarkson (eds), *Dictionary of Feminist Theologies*, Louisville: Westminster John Knox, p. 228.

ples to go out and do what he did; when they failed, he castigated them for their little faith (Matthew 10.1–4). At the end, the disciples were sent out to the world (Matthew 28.18–20) and given the spirit of power, enabling Christian believers to speak (Acts 2).

How, then, can we use prophecy as a method of teaching and fighting HIV/AIDS? I suggest the following:

- We need to show (or realize) that HIV/AIDS is a historical crisis for nations and the world as a whole, and that it violates God's will.
- We need to expound a firm prophetic theology that highlights the role of every Christian not to speak in judgement but to hope.
- We need to encourage students (and lecturers) to carry out a self-assessment on how they have been, or failed to be, prophetic in their own contexts, and to take a prophetic stance against all forms of social structures which promote injustice – which today is fertile soil for HIV/AIDS.
- We need to show students and congregations how the prophetic framework of our Christian faith enables us to face and deal with all the critical issues of HIV/AIDS prevention and care, such as healing, stigma, social exclusion, poverty, gender, youth powerlessness, the plight of orphans and widows, national and international injustice, and oppressive cultural beliefs.
- Our prophetic approach to teaching and preaching must also cover practical involvement of students. It must position trainee ministers and theological students in the communities, training them to meet with the suffering and express solidarity with them. It must teach them how to talk openly to those in power, be they leaders of their villages, churches or nations, if their policies, traditions, theologies and laws perpetrate oppression. We must train students to assume a prophetic stance in their work and in society.
- The sermons and liturgy of students must demonstrate that they are taking a prophetic role.

The time to assume our prophetic role in teaching, I would insist, is now.

7. AIDS, Leprosy and the Synoptic Jesus

ROBIN GILL

In seeking to make a theologically appropriate response to the challenge of AIDS today, a connection is frequently made with the response of the Synoptic Jesus to the challenge of leprosy. This connection is made explicitly, but in passing, in the Windhoek Report. It is also made in many thousands of other statements, articles and sermons (as an internet search soon reveals).[1] However, it has seldom been explored systematically. In this chapter I will argue that such exploration is both theologically important and instructive.

The connection is complicated by a widespread agreement among biblical scholars that 'leprosy' in the Bible (*sara'at* in the Jewish Bible or *lepra* in the New Testament) is not simply to be identified with Hansen's disease (*Elephantiasis Graecorum*).[2] Using his medical knowledge, S. G. Browne argued that none of the biblical references to leprosy includes 'any of the indubitable signs and symptoms of leprosy, and those that are mentioned tell against rather than for leprosy'. In addition,

---

1 I am most grateful to Jeff Astley for the observation that entering 'leprosy' and 'AIDS' together in an Advanced Google Search clearly demonstrates this connection.

2 See, for example, Vincent Taylor, 1959, *The Gospel According to St Mark*, London: Macmillan, p. 186; W. D. Davies and Dale C. Allison Jr, 1991, *A Critical Commentary on the Gospel According to St Matthew*, Vol. II, Edinburgh: T & T Clark, pp. 10–11; Martin Noth, 1965, *Leviticus*, London: SCM Press, p. 106; and Gordon J. Wenham, 1979, *The Book of Leviticus*, London: Hodder and Stoughton, p. 195.

'none of the pathognomonic features of leprosy are so much as hinted at: these are, anaesthetic areas of the skin, painless and progressive ulceration of the extremities, and facial nodules'.[3] So despite the tempting clinical association that is sometimes reported between leprosy (Hansen's disease) and AIDS in the modern world,[4] the theological connection has more to do with social perceptions than with epidemiology.

Once seen in terms of social perceptions, both biblical leprosy and modern-day AIDS have quite a number of startling and theologically significant similarities. Just as leprosy in the Bible was surrounded by social fears, interdictions and stigmatization that had little or no relation to aetiological medicine, so AIDS in the modern world has spawned similar social fears, interdictions and stigmatization – once again with little or no relation to aetiological medicine. And some of the cruder theological responses to disease and natural disaster illustrated by Job's critics in the Bible have sadly been replicated by some church leaders in the modern world.

Using the frame of social perception it is possible to construct a typology of leprosy, first in the Jewish Bible and then in the Synoptic Gospels. It is from a critical comparison of these two typologies that a more appropriate Christian theological response to AIDS might then be sought. This is not of course to maintain that social perceptions of biblical leprosy and modern-day AIDS are identical. Inescapably AIDS is strongly associated with sexual activity (even though, epidemiologically, HIV has often been contracted through needles and blood transfusions and transmitted from HIV-positive mothers to their babies) whereas biblical leprosy was not (albeit, as Mary Douglas points out, in Africa today 'leprosy is widely associated with incest').[5] It is sufficient to claim that there are some instructive social similarities between biblical leprosy and modern-day AIDS.

---

3 S. G. Browne, 1970, *Leprosy in the Bible*, London: Christian Medical Fellowship, p. 8.

4 The Indian Association of Leprologists reported an association between leprosy and AIDS at a clinical level: http://www.rediff.com/news/2004/nov/05med.htm.

5 Mary Douglas, 1999, *Leviticus as Literature*, Oxford: Oxford University Press, p. 185.

A tenfold typology of social perceptions of leprosy (*sara'at*) in the Jewish Bible (located particularly in the Priestly Code) might be constructed as follows.

First, *Leprosy is visibly shocking.* Moses (Exodus 4.6), Miriam (Numbers 12.10) and Gehazi (2 Kings 5.27) are all depicted as being 'leprous, as white as snow'. Wenham objects to the addition of 'white' in this translation and argues instead that 'the point of comparison may well be the flakiness of snow'.[6] Whether white or flaky, leprosy is regarded as visible and shocking (and different, of course, from the visibly shocking ulceration of the extremities and facial nodules characteristic of Hansen's disease).

Second, *Leprosy requires vigorous testing by the priest.* Leviticus 13 is the primary source for this testing. 'The priest shall examine the disease on the skin of his body, and if the hair in the diseased area has turned white and the disease appears to be deeper than the skin of his body, it is a leprous disease' (Leviticus 13.3). The priest must re-examine those suspected of leprosy seven days later to see if 'the disease is checked and . . . has not spread in the skin' (13.5) and again seven days later. As Martin Noth observes: 'It was the priest's business to pronounce on the state of cleanness and uncleanness; hence it is a case here of fixing the priestly professional knowledge in writing.'[7] Later Rabbinic texts discussed (a) whether the 'colours of leprosy signs' were sixteen, thirty-six or seventy-two and (b) whether priests should 'inspect leprosy-signs for the first time the day after the Sabbath, since [the end of] that week will fall on the Sabbath'.[8]

Third, *Leprosy involves (dangerous) impurity.* Mary Douglas emphasizes that not all forms of impurity depicted in the Priestly Code involve danger or deep disgust. But leprosy does: 'Leviticus certainly plays upon disgust at bodily exudations in its long disquisition on uncleanness of bleeding and leprosy . . . if impure was not originally a term of vilification it certainly has

---

6 Wenham, *The Book of Leviticus*, p. 195.

7 Noth, *Leviticus*, p. 103.

8 Jacob Neusner, 1971, *The Rabbinic Traditions About the Pharisees Before 70: Part I The Masters*, Leiden: E. J. Brill, p. 406.

become one.'⁹ 'The Lord spoke to Moses, saying: Command the Israelites to put out of the camp everyone who is leprous, or has a discharge, and everyone who is unclean through contact with a corpse . . . they must not defile their camp, where I dwell among them' (Numbers 5.1–3).

Fourth, *Lepers fearfully render other people/objects impure.* Leprosy can even affect a house (appearing as 'greenish or reddish spots' deeper than the surface of the walls) and 'the priest shall command that they empty the house before the priest goes to examine the disease, or all that is in the house will become unclean' (Leviticus 14.36). Mary Douglas again shows how leprosy is believed to spread, to defile and to become ever more dangerous. It starts with the postulating body, it then spreads to the garments, then to the house, and finally and disastrously to the tabernacle:

> If there is no cure, the incurably defiled house must be destroyed (Leviticus 14.39–42), as also the incurable leprous garment (Leviticus 13.52), and eventually the incurable leper can expect to be destroyed by the disease. In the last case, defilement of the tabernacle, chapter 16 enjoins the rite of atonement for the tabernacle. If defilement of the tabernacle were not remedied, the people could expect the curses of chapter 26 to be unleashed upon them as a punishment for failing to keep the covenant.¹⁰

Fifth, *Leprosy can result from sin.* In three of the leprosy stories in the Jewish Bible the disease does seem to be associated with sinful behaviour resulting in God's anger or the anger of God's representatives. Miriam angered God for speaking against Moses (Numbers 12.8), Gehazi angered Elisha because of his greed (2 Kings 5.25) and King Uzziah angered the priests because he rather than they made an offering (2 Chronicles 26.19).

Sixth, *Leprosy is inflicted by God.* Even when such sinful behaviour does not seem to be associated with leprosy, the

9 Douglas, *Leviticus as Literature*, p. 145.
10 Douglas, *Leviticus as Literature*, pp. 191–2.

disease is still inflicted by God. So in the Moses leprosy story, the Lord said to Moses, '"Put your hand inside your cloak." He put his hand into his cloak; and when he took it out, his hand was leprous, as white as snow' (Exodus 4.6). Again, in Leviticus, 'The LORD spoke to Moses and Aaron saying: When you come into the land of Canaan, which I give you for a possession, and I put a leprous disease in a house . . . ' (Leviticus 14.33–34). And in the Uzziah story, although it did involve sin, the king 'was leprous in his forehead . . . because the Lord had struck him' (2 Chronicles 26.20).

Seventh, *Leprosy requires extensive reparation*. Whether leprosy involves sinful behaviour or not, it does require priestly reparation, set out in great detail in Leviticus 14: 'The priest shall offer the sin-offering, to make atonement for the one to be cleansed from his uncleanness. Afterwards he shall slaughter the burnt offering' (Leviticus 14.19).

Eighth, *Leprosy necessitates social exclusion, interdictions and stigmatization*. Leviticus 13 is again the primary source, supplying a recipe for the social exclusion and stigmatization of lepers for many centuries to come: 'The person who has the leprous disease shall wear torn clothes and let the hair of his head be dishevelled; and he shall cover his upper lip and cry out, "Unclean, unclean." He shall remain unclean as long as he has the disease; he is unclean. He shall live alone; his dwelling shall be outside the camp' (Leviticus 13.45–46). The leper is of course a source of dangerous impurity to other people, to buildings and, especially, to the tabernacle (and, in medieval Europe, to church buildings). Emphatically lepers 'must not defile their camp, where I dwell among them' (Numbers 5.3). Royal status was no exception; even King Uzziah 'being leprous lived in a separate house, for he was excluded from the house of the LORD' (2 Chronicles 26.21).

Ninth, *Leprosy consumes flesh uncontrollably*. Aaron pleads with Moses on behalf of Miriam: 'Do not let her be like one stillborn, whose flesh is half consumed when it comes out of its mother's womb' (Numbers 12.12).

Tenth, *Leprosy can remain until (and even beyond) death*. Gehazi is told by Elisha: 'Therefore the leprosy of Naaman shall cling to you, and to your descendants for ever' (2 Kings 5.27) and 'King Uzziah was leprous to the day of his death' (2 Chronicles 26.21).

Not all of this tenfold typology relates to social perceptions of AIDS today, but much of it does, especially in parts of sub-Sahara where HIV inflection is so tragically rife. In parts of Africa today AIDS is depicted as 'slims' disease because of the shocking physical degeneration of many suffers; it is widely regarded as a dangerous impurity – albeit an impurity that might be removed by sleeping with virgins or by remedies supplied by traditional (priestly) healers; it is closely associated with sin, and viewed (even by some church leaders) as a punishment from God; it is believed to necessitate social exclusion, interdictions and stigmatization; as 'slims' disease it consumes flesh uncontrollably – and of course it can remain at least until death.

Within Western countries, too, especially in the 1980s when AIDS was still widely seen as 'the gay disease', some of these social perceptions were present. Against medical explanations at the time, HIV was widely regarded as contagious to touch (Princess Diana's hugging of a small child with AIDS is often depicted as an iconic breaking of this social perception) and some deemed AIDS to be God's punishment of homosexuality. Members of the gay community sought anonymous testing precisely because they feared exclusion and stigmatization by society at large. And only the effectiveness of cocktails of anti-retroviral drugs in recent years has reduced apocalyptic fears of early or untimely death.

Allied to this there have frequently been public (even government) denials based upon social perceptions rather than upon rigorous empirical research: denials of a link between HIV infection and AIDS disease; denials that a particular country or church had any prevalence of HIV infection (or even of any homosexuals); denials that unprotected heterosexual (rather than homosexual) intercourse also spreads HIV infection; and denials by individuals that they have been party to this spread of HIV inflection. Social exclusion, stigmatization and a lack of truth-telling have all too often been responses to the challenge of AIDS.

How does this social perception of *sara'at* in the Jewish Bible compare with that of *lepra* in the Synoptic Gospels? There are six discrete mentions of the disease in the Synoptic Gospels, and none elsewhere in the New Testament. The most elusive of these is the mention of Jesus being 'in the house of Simon the leper' when a woman anoints him with costly ointment (Mark 14.3 and Matthew 26.6). John Nolland argues that 'it is most natural to think in terms of Simon as someone whose identity is expected to be known in the Christian folk memory of the Gospel readership, and who is remembered as one cured of leprosy by Jesus'.[11] Vincent Taylor suggests more vaguely that this house 'must have been known to the circle from which the story comes'.[12] In Matthew the 12 disciples are charged to 'cure the sick, raise the dead, cleanse the lepers, cast out demons' (10.8). In both Matthew and Luke (significantly adding the reference to lepers to the original quotation from Isaiah) John the Baptist's disciples are told to report back that 'the blind receive their sight, the lame walk, the lepers are cleansed, the deaf hear, the dead are raised, and the poor have good news brought to them' (Matthew 11.5 and Luke 7.22). Then there are two extended leper stories. There is the story of the cleansing of the leper contained in all three Synoptic Gospels (Mark 1.40–45; Matthew 8.1–4; Luke 5.12–16). And there is the story of the ten lepers recounted only by Luke (17.11–19).

The fascinating sixth allusion to leprosy, given only in Luke – Jesus (in a story foundational for Liberation theology) declared in the synagogue: 'There were also many lepers in Israel in the time of the prophet Elisha, and none of them was cleansed except Naaman the Syrian' (Luke 4.27) – suggests an illuminating typology for these leprosy stories and depictions. Setting out the Elisha/Naaman story in eight phases – Prelude, Prophet's Initial Response, Encounter, Required Ritual, Cleansed Leper's Return, Prophet's Response, Dismissal and Follow-up – clear Synoptic parallels can be seen with all but the last. And even the last may have a parallel in the broader Lucan corpus.

---

11 John Nolland, 2005, *The Gospel of Matthew*, Grand Rapids, MN: William B. Eerdmans, p. 1051.

12 Taylor, *The Gospel According to St Mark*, p. 530.

Prelude

In the Elisha/Naaman story the latter, in contrast to the prophet himself, is depicted as being a 'commander of the army of the king of Aram . . . a great man and in high favour with his master' (2 Kings 5.1). Yet, of course, 'the man, though a mighty warrior, suffered from leprosy'. None of the lepers that feature in the Synoptic stories are depicted in this way (unless Nolland's supposition about 'Simon the leper' is extended). However, in Matthew the centurion in the story immediately following his main leper story is similarly depicted as 'a man under authority, with soldiers under me; and I say to one, 'Go,' and he goes, and to another, 'Come,' and he comes, and to my slave, 'Do this,' and the slave does it' (Matthew 8.9).

Prophet's initial response

Elisha's initial response to hearing about Naaman's plight was, 'Let him come to me, that he may learn that there is a prophet in Israel' (2 Kings 5.8). Similarly the Synoptic Jesus responded: 'Go and tell John [the Baptist] what you hear and see: the blind receive their sight; the lame walk; the lepers are cleansed . . . What did you come out to see? A prophet?' (Matthew 11.4ff.; Luke 7.22ff.).

Encounter

Naaman came to Elisha with chariots and gifts, whereas Elisha issued a command from within his house without meeting him. Similarly, the ten lepers are depicted as 'keeping their distance' from Jesus (Luke 17.12) and the centurion's servant is healed at a distance (Matthew 8.5f.).

Required ritual

Elisha required Naaman to 'Go, wash in the Jordan seven times, and your flesh shall be restored and you shall be clean' (2 Kings

5.10). In the two Synoptic extended stories both the single leper and the ten lepers are commanded to go to the priest(s) in accord with the rituals required in Leviticus 13 and 14: 'See that you say nothing to anyone; but go, show yourself to the priest, and offer for your cleansing what Moses commanded, as a testimony to them' (Mark 1.44) and 'Go and show yourselves to the priests' (Luke 17.14).

Cleansed leper's return

Naaman, an Aramean, freshly cleansed, 'returned to the man of God, he and all his company; he came and stood before him and said, "Now I know that there is no God in all the earth except in Israel; please accept a present from your servant"' (2 Kings 5.15). In the extended Luke story, one of the ten lepers, a Samaritan, 'when he saw that he was healed, turned back, praising God with a loud voice. He prostrated himself at Jesus' feet and thanked him' (Luke 17.15–16).

Prophet's response

Elisha would accept no payment from Naaman: 'As the LORD lives, whom I serve, I will accept nothing!' (2 Kings 5.16). And in the Synoptic Gospels the disciples were told by Jesus to 'give without payment' (Matthew 10.8), and a leper was told to say 'nothing to anyone' (Mark 1.44; Matthew 8.4; Luke 5.14).

Dismissal

Elisha said to the cured Naaman, 'Go in peace' (2 Kings 5.19). In Luke, Jesus said to one of the ten cured lepers: 'Get up and go on your way; your faith has made you well' (Luke 17.19).

Follow-up

In the (perhaps added) sequel to the Elisha/Naaman story Gehazi was chastised by Elisha because of his financial deception: 'the leprosy of Naaman shall cling to you, and to your descendants, for ever' (2 Kings 5.27). A very tentative parallel might be made with Ananias and Sapphira being chastised by Peter because of their financial deception: 'How is it that you have agreed together to put the Spirit of the Lord to the test? Look, the feet of those who have buried your husband are at the door, and they will carry you out' (Acts 5.9).

Yet, despite the many parallels suggested by this typology there are also some crucial and highly instructive differences between the Elisha/Naaman story and the leprosy stories and depictions in the Synoptic Gospels. Jesus' very declaration in the synagogue that 'There were also many lepers in Israel in the time of the prophet Elisha, and none of them was cleansed except Naaman the Syrian' (Luke 4.27) is followed (not very logically, suggests Christopher Evans[13]) by a threat of violence from those in the synagogue: 'They got up, drove him out of the town, and led him to the brow of the hill on which their town was built, so that they might hurl him off the cliff' (Luke 4.29). In the Elisha/Naaman story no violence is directed against the prophet, despite Naaman's anger at the prophet's required ritual. Violence is rather directed in the sequel by the prophet himself at his greedy servant, just as earlier he had directed extreme violence on 42 boys who had 'jeered at him, saying, "Go away, baldhead! Go away, baldhead!"' (2 Kings 2.23).

Another important difference is that the required ritual action (at a distance from Elisha) effects the cleansing of Naaman from leprosy: 'So [Naaman] went down and immersed himself seven times in the Jordan, according to the word of the man of God; his flesh was restored like the flesh of a young boy, and he was clean' (2 Kings 5.14). In contrast, in the two extended leper stories in the Synoptic Gospels the cleansing takes place in the presence of Jesus, and the required ritual to go

---

13 C. F. Evans, 1990, *Saint Luke*, London and Philadelphia: SCM Press and Trinity Press, p. 275.

to 'the priest' is not in order to be cleansed of the leprosy but in order to be pronounced clean (as required by Leviticus 13).

Most important of all, in a context of seeking a theologically appropriate response to the challenge of AIDS today, the cleansing in the Synoptic stories involves direct touching by Jesus. Elisha, while keeping his distance, issued a command from inside his house through a messenger to Naaman the leper outside. Only when the latter had been cleansed at a distance was it that 'he returned to the man of God, he and all his company; he came and stood before him' (2 Kings 5.15). In contrast, the ten lepers approach Jesus directly, albeit 'keeping their distance', calling out, 'Jesus, Master have mercy on us!' (Luke 17.12). Jesus sees them and responds to them directly. Even more striking, in the other extended story in all three Synoptic Gospels Jesus responded to the leper's plea for compassion and 'stretched out his hand and touched' the leper (Mark 1.41; Matthew 8.3; Luke 5.13). Luke's version of the story is particularly vivid (the words in italics are unique to Luke):

> Once, when he was in one of the cities, there was a man *covered with leprosy.* When he saw Jesus, he *bowed with his face to the ground* and begged him, 'Lord, if you choose, you can make me clean.' Then Jesus stretched out his hand, touched him, and said, 'I do choose. Be made clean.' Immediately the leprosy left him. (Luke 5.12–13)

I have sought to show elsewhere just how important is this combination of responding to a plea for compassion and touching the one perceived to be so unclean, especially in the context of AIDS today.[14] It is also central to Margaret Farley, Musa Dube and others here. If there is a single element in the Synoptic healing stories that has attracted responsible Christian commentators it is precisely this. In sermons posted on the internet it is noted again and again. One, for example, from a minister of the Faithful Central Bible Church argues, passionately (albeit confusing Matthew and Luke) that

---

14 See my 2006 *Health Care and Christian Ethics*, Cambridge: Cambridge University Press, chapter 5.

I suggest that if we understand Jesus' attitude about leprosy, the AIDS of His day, we will know how we ought to respond to it. Let the position and posture of Jesus be your position and posture as you deal with the issue of AIDS. The account of the incident in the book of Matthew says the man was 'full of leprosy,' which means he was in the final stages of the disease. He was dying, and praise the Lord, Jesus did not waste time satisfying his curiosity or passing judgment. The man needed help . . . He saw to the man's need.[15]

The Jesuit Kenneth Overberg makes a similar, albeit more sophisticated, theological point in seeking to develop 'a biblical vision of AIDS':

> Jesus . . . crosses the boundaries of purity laws to touch the alienated . . . with a simple touch, Jesus breaks down the barriers, challenges customs and laws that alienate, and embodies his convictions about the inclusive meaning of the reign of God (Mark 1.40–42) . . . This event not only reveals Jesus' care for an individual in need but also his concern about structures of society. Jesus steps across the boundaries separating the unclean and actually touches the leper. In doing so, Jesus enters into the leper's isolation and becomes unclean.[16]

Biblical scholars might rightly sound a note of caution about such connections. James Dunn, for example, warns that 'we cannot say that Jesus touched the leper (Mark 1.41) in defiance of the purity code. And the probable testimony of 1.44 is that Jesus instructed the leper to follow the required procedure for a person with a contagious skin disease to be readmitted to society. In which case Jesus acted in accord with the purity laws.'[17] For Dunn, 'the point is rather that Jesus seems to disregard the impurity consequences in such cases, so that it may be fairly

---

15 http://healingbeginshere.org/sermon/kculmer_sermon.htm.

16 http://www.americancatholic.org/Newsletters/SFS/an1098.asp.

17 James D. G. Dunn, 2002, 'Jesus and Purity: An Ongoing Debate', *New Testament Studies* 48, p. 461.

concluded that Jesus was indifferent to such purity issues'.[18] For the present theological connection this is probably sufficient. The Synoptic Jesus does indeed seem to disregard the impurity consequences of *lepra*. In this respect he differs sharply from crucial aspects of the tenfold typology based upon social perceptions of *sara'at* in the Jewish Bible. The Synoptic Jesus also differs, despite many other similarities, specifically from the Elisha/Naaman story. Jesus touches the unclean leper, but Elisha does not (neither did the priests in Leviticus nor the rabbis subsequently). More than that, the Synoptic Jesus' touching is a direct and personal response to a plea for compassion.

Amidst all the continuities between these biblical stories, these discontinuities are theologically crucial in the context of AIDS today. Learning to disregard (socially perceived) impurity consequences is essential for developing an appropriate theological response to AIDS, just as it was essential to Jesus to disregard the dire impurity consequences of *lepra*. The tenfold typology demonstrates just how dire the latter were for those nurtured within the priestly code of the Jewish Bible. *Lepra* then and AIDS in much of Africa today are both visibly shocking, involve dangerous and defiling impurity, are deemed to be inflicted by God characteristically as punishment for sin, necessitate social exclusion, interdictions and stigmatization, consume flesh uncontrollably and signal early death, leaving children as orphans and the elderly without carers. Yet the Synoptic Jesus, moved by compassion or responding to pleas for compassion, habitually disregarded such consequences when approached by those deemed to be impure by the priestly code. Even if the Synoptic Jesus is considered to be an otherwise observant Jew, instructing cleansed lepers to follow the rituals required in Leviticus 13 and 14, he still allows compassion to trump deeply embedded scruples about dangerous and defiling impurity.

Herein I believe lies one of the sharpest theological challenges both to much secular ethics and to a number of versions of Christian ethics. As I have argued elsewhere,[19] within the

---

18 Dunn, 'Jesus and Purity', p. 461.
19 See my *Health Care and Christian Ethics*, pp. 94ff.

Synoptic healing stories compassion is not simply about feeling sorry for the vulnerable, nor is it even just about empathy, a preparedness to identify with the vulnerable. Rather, compassion is both a response to the vulnerable and a determination to help them, sometimes at the expense of principled scruples. That exactly expresses what I believe is the proper theological response to the challenge of AIDS.

8. AIDS and Theological Education

DENISE M. ACKERMANN

Whatever we say, analyse and critique, we must do so in hope. Hope is the antidote to the despair bred by stigma. Stigma produces social inequality. It is deployed by concrete social actors who seek to legitimize their own dominant status. It therefore operates on a religious and political economy of exclusion, often at the point of intersection between culture, power and difference. Stigma rarely functions exclusively in relation to HIV and AIDS. When culture, gender, race and sexual stigmas work together with stigmas engendered by HIV and AIDS, the effects are complex and often devastating. For example: AIDS is seen as either the disease of the rich or the poor, depending on one's class perspective; or AIDS is a women's disease, or a disease caused by men, depending again on one's gender perspective; or AIDS is a black disease or a white issue, depending on one's race perspective; and so on. As theologians seek to grapple with difference, we find out just how profoundly stigma – in its many guises – permeates all of life.

Theological education should be devoted to the critical academic pursuit of the theological disciplines. It is, however, also theology done in service of our communities of faith. It combines academic knowledge with a compelling interest in the activities of communities of faith and their relationship with their contexts. It is not solely a quest for knowledge: it is also about meaning and the pursuit of truth in our lives.

When faced with the challenge of teaching in a context that is deeply affected by HIV and AIDS, lecturers resort to a variety of inappropriate approaches. Feeling ill-equipped to deal with the topic of AIDS and having not given sufficient attention to the theological implications of HIV and AIDS, the 'one-off' or 'add-on' approach is resorted to. The local university AIDS bureau is invited to send an 'expert' to give a one-day update on what is happening in the fields of HIV and AIDS and to speak about prevention. After the expert departs, the students are subjected to a quick theological gloss and the matter is then considered closed.

A second approach is the 'new sensitivity mode'. A faculty dean earnestly instructs lecturers to incorporate HIV and AIDS into the teaching of all their subjects in some way or other. This is similar to earlier efforts to incorporate gender sensitivity into teaching when lecturers were told to use inclusive language and to be aware of the implications of gender for their disciplines. Most lecturers are baffled about how to apply the 'new sensitivity mode'. After numerous attempts it is usually quietly shelved.

A third approach is the 'immersion experience'. The professor of pastoral theology takes a group of students off for a day to 'immerse' them into the experience of suffering caused by HIV and AIDS. Hospitals, hospices or homes are visited and people are interviewed. By the end of the day, the students are completely overwhelmed, often because they have not been sufficiently prepared for these encounters. This approach is heavily focused on practice, with little theoretical backing. These three approaches are clearly caricatured, but I have experienced all of them in some form or other.

Theological education which takes the challenge of HIV and AIDS seriously will have to re-conceptualize the theological curriculum. Why? Because HIV and AIDS and its related stigmas impinge on virtually every aspect of the theological curriculum. Our doctrines of God, sin and salvation, our understanding of suffering, the nature of the human being and the nature of the Church are all, for instance, related to our struggle to live faithfully in contexts ravaged by suffering and death, exacerbated by stubborn stigmas. As central as theoretical knowledge is to the academic pursuit, I do not want to overemphasize its role. As I have said, I do believe that theological education is done in service of our communities of faith. This calls for specific attention to be paid, on the one hand, to the relationship between our theoretical knowledge and belief systems, and, on the other hand, to the way in which knowledge translates into actions and shapes them.

In order to hold the tension between our theological theories and our Christian practices, I suggest that we theological educators examine our theological methodology. How many of us are still working with a *depositum fidei* method? This method assumes that theological knowledge is received from on high and that theological educators are to play the role of enlightened go-betweens imparting it to students. There are other ways of teaching theology that are more effective in dealing with HIV and AIDS and their related stigmas.

First, there is the critical role of narrative in disseminating knowledge. Life stories are important in countering stigma. Telling stories is critical in claiming one's identity. Instead of having one's identity subsumed under the label of being 'an HIV-positive', speaking and being heard affirms both dignity and identity. Narrative has a further function: the very act of telling our stories helps us to make sense of situations that are often incomprehensible – even chaotic. The need to counter stigma and deal with HIV and AIDS in a theologically responsible manner begins with lived experience. When our stories intersect with the meta-narrative of our faith – the life, ministry, death and resurrection of Jesus Christ – despair can give way to hope, and God's caring presence can be affirmed, even in the midst of trying circumstances.

Second, theological methodology must be alive to the creative tension between theory and praxis. Too often praxis is seen as subsidiary to theory. Praxis has to do with the interconnectedness of historical experience and the concerns for freedom on the one hand, and our responsibility to change oppressive conditions into the possibility of human flourishing, on the other. Such praxis is done in the interest of those who experience stigma. It is collaborative by nature, and it is culturally sensitive to the different ways of experiencing reality. Christian praxis is a willingness to be God's hands in the world.

Third, an appropriate theological methodology requires critical analysis. The need to understand the relationship between, for instance, culture, religion and gender, or between knowledge and power, or the challenge that difference poses to theological education, all point to how essential critical analytical thinking is for the theological enterprise.

To illustrate the point, I want to refer to a critical analysis done by an African woman theologian at a conference on AIDS in Pretoria in 1998. Teresa Okure stated that there are two viruses that are more important than HIV. The audience reacted with shock. She proceeded to explain that the first virus is one that stigmatizes and demeans women in society. This virus causes men to abuse women. It is the virus that is responsible for the shocking fact that in many countries in Africa the condition that carries the highest risk of HIV infection is that of being a married woman. HIV and AIDS thrive on disordered gender relations. It is the virus which is deadly for the poor woman who lives in a patriarchal relationship and has little power over what happens to her body. The second virus that enables HIV and AIDS to spread at a devastating speed is found mostly in the developed world. It is the virus of global economic injustice that causes terrible poverty in parts of the developing world. Capitalist market economies are thrust on societies that are not geared for them and structural adjustment programmes imposed that do not meet the needs of the poor, who too often consist of uneducated, rural women and their dependants.

Having asserted that HIV and AIDS challenge us in virtually all fields of theological education, I want to suggest how we might reframe our theological thinking on two well-known theological topics in order to deal more appropriately with HIV- and AIDS-related stigma.

First, we are challenged by the constant theme that underlies all debates on HIV and AIDS – the question of how we understand human sexuality and its place in our teaching of theological anthropology. What does it mean to be a sexual human being? The Church is a community of sexual beings who find sexual expression in different ways. Sexuality challenges us to confront difference. It also challenges us to acknowledge the centrality of the body in our theological thinking. All reality and all knowledge are mediated through our bodies. We do not live disembodied lives. Our bodies are more than skin, bones and flesh. The fact that we can see, hear, touch, smell and feel is the source of what we know. The nonsense that the body is secondary to the soul has plagued Christian history for too long and must be countered with embodied theological thinking. Thus theology that takes human sexuality seriously pays attention to the nature of the human being as created by God, and the nature of our relationships with one another as expressions of our humanity in its fullness. Emphasizing the call to mutual, caring relationships and the fact that human sexuality is a gift from God, are both important when dealing with stigma and discrimination. It is strange that Christians, whose faith is grounded in Incarnate Love, are so reluctant to grapple with what it means to have bodies.

Second, we are challenged by our lack of an effective language to deal with HIV and stigma. Stigma is nourished by silence. Internalized trauma, fear of rejection, cultural restraints and wrong understandings of sin and punishment – all rob people of the ability to speak out and to name their reality. I suggest that our scriptures have given us a language that can deal with suffering. In the ancient language of lament we have a way of naming the unnameable and of crying out to God in situations that are unbearable. What is lament? It is a form of mourning but it is more purposeful. It signals that relationships have gone terribly wrong and it reminds God that God must act as a partner in the covenant. It is both individual and communal. It is a primal cry that comes out of the human soul and beats against the heart of God. It calls God to account for our human suffering. Lament is risky and dangerous speech; it is restless; it pushes the boundaries of our relationships, particularly with God; it refuses to settle for things the way they are. Israel knew the power of lament. The Psalms bear witness to this as they express the rawness of human suffering as well as hope and trust in God. Israel discovered that lament and praise go hand in hand.

When the language of lament is applied in our present context, it has important implications for the political and social witness of the Church. The Church claims to be an inclusive and caring community. Why is it not publicly lamenting the devastation caused by HIV and AIDS? Lament can be politically subversive and therefore dangerous. It is never for the preservation of the *status quo*. This is the challenge to our churches – to lament the present suffering. Lament can also enrich our liturgies and pastoral care. Liturgical praise often comes too easily. It is not praise that is hard won and that names the truth to God while confirming that God will hear our cries and will act to bring relief. The language of lament is also a powerful pastoral tool for dealing with suffering. Lastly, lament makes for a more intimate and authentic relationship with God. We live in a situation that raises legitimate questions about God's justice and God's power and presence in a suffering world. Is God's justice reliable and where is God? There is much cause for lament, yet its loss stifles our questions about evil in the world. Instead we settle for a God who is covered in a sugar-coated veneer of religious optimism, whose omnipotence will 'make everything right in the end'. Religious optimism differs deeply from the life of faith. The former prefers to sanitize God by removing God from the ugliness of suffering. This is a God we dare not approach with our genuine grief and with whom we are in a relationship of eternal infantilism.

The language of lament is direct and truthful about suffering; it names the unnameable to God and in so doing helps to heal our doubts and restore our faith in our power to call on God to act on our cries. Why not teach our students about the richness of the tradition of lament as a means of countering the pain of HIV- and AIDS-related stigma?

I agree with those who have said that HIV and AIDS constitute a time of *kairos*. This takes me back to the Kairos Document which appeared in South Africa in 1985. The first few phrases went something like: 'The time has come, the moment of truth has arrived, and South Africa has been plunged into a crisis that is shaking its foundations . . .' These words have a new and startling relevance now.

This is a moment of truth. It encompasses crisis and opportunity, despair and hope, struggle and grace. It is in the very nature of our profound crisis that I find hope – hope in the Holy One who has promised to be with us always. Finally, this *kairos* requires that we should nurture a spirituality that breathes the air of hope, is unafraid of ambiguity, is ready for works of justice and charity, but also takes time to reflect on what we should be doing. Then hearts can change and hands can become willing tools in hastening the coming of God's reign on earth.

9. Evangelicals and AIDS

STAN NUSSBAUM

Concerns and assumptions

In the face of the horrid pandemic of HIV/AIDS, we make the following assumptions, which we believe are increasingly shared by churches and Christian faith-based organizations around the world:

- The human race has AIDS. It is not 'their' problem. It is our problem as members of the race. If it is not our problem, we are not human.
- Despite the fact that the virus was first identified in the North, Christians in the global South are far ahead of the North on understanding and dealing with it as one aspect of their wider mission. They have years of battle experience.
- The local congregational contribution to the HIV/AIDS battle, especially the non-quantifiable aspects of it, is not readily visible to Christians in the North. When they think of the 'Christian' contribution, they may think primarily of the programmes of large Christian NGOs and missions, not the everyday ministry of congregations.
- The local congregational contribution is often not recognized by governments and local secular groups battling HIV/AIDS. Relations between church-based and secular groups are improving but not yet as positive as they need to be for optimal teamwork and maximal effectiveness.
- The world and the Church are at last waking up to the AIDS crisis, but amid the deluge of information about the HIV/

AIDS pandemic, relatively little is specifically oriented to help church and mission leaders.[1]

One of many examples of the wake-up call is the AIDS Declaration of the Holistic Mission Study Group given at the Forum of the Lausanne Congress on World Evangelization, held in September 2004, which states: 'Many African churches have taken the lead in responding in prevention and care. A few Asian churches are doing the same. Churches in other parts of the world have been slower to respond. *What is missing is global commitment on the part of all evangelicals* to provide what God has given them to the fight against this scourge' (italics added).[2]

Increasing the capacity of congregations for HIV/AIDS ministry

The reports (the term 'country report' used in this chapter is the primary document each local researcher submitted to the project) and email dialogue throughout this present project have led me to the conclusion that the two main internal challenges of the congregations are, first, the practical challenge of recruiting, training and sustaining volunteers and second, the more fundamental theological challenge of grasping the implications that the essence of the Christian message has for the HIV/AIDS challenge. Further, my assumption is that the first challenge will virtually take care of itself if the second challenge is met. Conversely, no matter how sophisticated our recruiting techniques become, most Christians will remain largely unmotivated, uninvolved and unrecruitable for HIV/AIDS ministry until a new vision of the Christian message turns them into radically transformed disciples of the Messiah.

---

1 The best introduction is Tetsunao Yamamori *et al.* (eds), 2003, *The Hope Factor: Engaging the Church in the HIV/AIDS Crisis*, Waynesboro, GA: Authentic Media.

2 Under 'Documents' on www.lausanne.org; see 'Holistic Mission: Occasional Paper No. 33'.

In other words, I am assuming that the reason why recruiting, training and sustaining volunteers is so difficult is that so many Christians, both in the North and in the South, have only a superficial understanding of the big picture of their own faith. Here we can only sketch three of the most relevant aspects of that big picture: a dynamic understanding of the core message of Christianity, a bias for the poor and suffering, and a positive theology of sexuality and gender. All three of these help to ignite, equip and encourage HIV/AIDS ministry by congregations. If that is correct, then theologians and teachers at all levels should spell out these and similar themes in appropriate ways in their own cultural settings, thus making their crucial contribution to the mobilization of the Church globally against HIV/AIDS.

A dynamic understanding of the core message of Christianity

In countries with a high prevalence of HIV/AIDS, the disease has exposed a crisis of faith and discipleship among Christians, namely this: the sexual lives of people who claim to have accepted a life-transforming gospel are not transformed. These untransformed people are superficial Christians, and there are millions of them.

They should not be confused with 'nominal' Christians, who often have nothing to do with their church except for rites of passage.[3] By contrast, the superficial Christians may be heavily involved in their churches. They may sing sincerely, they may pray sincerely, they may give money and time to their congregations, but all this has not translated into their everyday discipleship, especially in the areas of sexual behaviour and the practice of stigmatizing certain people.

---

3 The 'nominal' Christians also are not transformed, but it is much harder for the Church to influence their behaviour because they keep their distance. By contrast, the superficial Christians are constantly hearing church teaching and interacting with other members, and thus should be reachable with a transforming message.

The prime theological challenge of congregations is therefore to turn superficial Christians into deep, genuine Christians, to get them to exchange their static view of the good news for a dynamic, life-transforming one. As John Downing, the respondent from Kenya, put it, 'That is where the problem lies. All of the people who have responded to your survey and all our SPILL (St Paul's Institute for Life-long Learning) students, I would dare to claim, were sincerely into the area of radical discipleship. It is getting the message out beyond there [into the wider Christian community] that is the challenge.'

The dynamic good news we are speaking of is not an idea but an announcement: 'A new power is in operation!' (Romans 8.2). This power changes people from the inside out, transforming them totally though not instantly. No aspect of life is left untouched. The country report from India describes this as follows:

> Vision: To see every person complete in Christ. We long to see the church lovely, beautiful, free and full of the amazing life and glory of our living God. Where people are healed, where the lame walk, the blind see, the deaf hear! Where there is a life-changing encounter with Jesus . . . We believe that God's plan for restoration for the region will involve righteous people reaching out to the disempowered and the marginalized [including PLHA (people living with HIV/AIDS)]. True apostolic Christianity is always about remembering them (Galatians 2.10).

As part of that transformation or restoration, people become conscious of the mission they share. In Bosch's oft-quoted definition, mission is 'the participation of Christians in the liberating mission of Jesus, wagering on a future that verifiable experience seems to belie. It is the good news of God's love, incarnated in the witness of a community, for the sake of the world.'[4] In our era of a thousand distractions, the terrible AIDS pandemic has the wonderful effect of concentrating the mind of

---

4 David J. Bosch, 1991, *Transforming Mission*, Maryknoll, NY: Orbis, p. 519.

the Church on that mission. According to the country report from Honduras, that is what is needed so the Church can meet the HIV/AIDS needs it is not meeting yet, 'A wider church vision and mission in order to comply with the vision and mission of heaven.'

If more Christians would catch that vision and understand the Christian good news of the arriving power of God as something that governs and transforms their whole selves and all their social relationships, HIV would have a much harder time ever getting a strong foothold in a nation. HIV awareness campaigns, when they eventually come, would find a solid foundation on which to build – transformed people who already have their views of sexuality, gender, poverty and the like, shaped by the arriving reign of God. In a community of such people, an AIDS activist should find a lot of ready-made friends and allies from the beginning. The capacity of the churches would be many times easier to tap than it is today.

A bias for the poor and suffering

Whatever attitude one has toward suffering people in general is likely to be the same attitude one has toward people living with HIV/AIDS (PLHA). Those who are callous about poor people are likely also to be callous about PLHA. Reducing the thickness of those calluses is a problem for everyone who is mobilizing people to join the fight against AIDS.

The churches have a major role to play in re-sensitizing the de-sensitized. Their primary starting point is not to focus on the pathetic aspects of HIV/AIDS[5] but rather to call attention to the fact that the God of ancient Israel, unlike most other gods

---

5 The difference between a need-driven concept of mission and a kingdom-driven, Messiah-centred mission is well summed up in Tim Dearborn, 1999, 'Beyond Duty' in Ralph D. Winter and Steven C. Hawthorne (eds), *Perspective on the World Christian Movement*, 3rd edn, Pasadena: William Carey Library, pp. 90–3. The need-driven concept is the secular version, often mistakenly adopted by Christian groups. Dearborn explains how this leads to compassion fatigue, and why a Messiah-centred motivation for mission does not.

ancient and modern, has an explicit bias toward aiding widows, orphans and others for whom the prevailing world system does not work (Deuteronomy 26.12).

It is utterly hypocritical for Christians to identify ourselves with this God but not with his agenda. And this agenda cannot be quarantined in the Old Testament. It is amplified rather than muted in the New, in passages such as Matthew 25.31–46, the parable of the sheep and goats. Christians trying to mobilize other Christians for the HIV/AIDS battle therefore have a running start. Kurai Chitima from Zimbabwe writes in an e-mail: 'AIDS is not demanding something new of us Christians but that we really become the people we are called to be – people who share Jesus' love, power and hope to everyone.' The country report from Zambia states: 'The church, nation-wide, must be sensitised to see HIV/AIDS as an opportunity for it to show the love and compassion of the Lord Jesus Christ, thereby preaching the good news to the sick and other needy people.'

This sensitivity is already evident among many of the Christians in our study. When asked what motivated them to become involved and stay involved in HIV/AIDS work, they said things like, 'I was motivated by compassion after seeing the need of the affected persons. It's been rough running a faith-based organization without financial support like other secular organizations but the grace of God has kept me going' (the country report from Nigeria). Such people are the kind of people who will throw themselves into the battle at all levels, increasing the army's capacity.

A positive yet disciplined theology of sexuality

The crucial importance of breaking stigma has been emphasized in this report. This is no easy task since the process of stigmatization is deeply rooted in cultural understandings of sexuality, gender and disease. They often promote stigmatization or at least inhibit the open discussion that would allow the pattern of stigmatization to be broken. Thus they promote the spread of HIV/AIDS and will continue to do so until they are dealt with and replaced.

What do the churches have to contribute to replacing these deadly aspects of cultures? What are the liberating, life-giving Christian views of sexuality, gender and disease? In all countries in our sample group, articulating and promoting these views appeared to be a weak area. The churches are not yet operating with a well-developed theology of sexuality that relates it to the transforming power of the Messiah. For example, an email from Kenya says, 'In the Kenyan context the ambivalence on this issue is almost total. Sexuality is hardly discussed.' Similarly an email from Nigeria reports, 'The propriety of discussing sexuality in the church is a very controversial issue. Many are very hypocritical about it. Sexuality is often trivialised, supposedly because it is merely a physical thing and the important things in life are spiritual.'

Along what lines may the needed theology be developed? The Kenyan programme called SPILL (St Paul's Institute for Lifelong Learning) addresses this as follows:

> We see the SPILL role as dealing with these issues head on; ensuring that students can talk unashamedly about their and their community's sexuality. To be analytical, critical and self-critical. But above all to make the paradigm shift to a New Covenant model of sexuality . . . [The model relates to the] doctrines of the two humanities: on the one hand born and bound in Adam-humanity, but on the other hand re-born and liberated into Messiah humanity. Only in this latter state does the human become truly human. In this latter redeemed humanity, the theology of sexuality needs to be defined and celebrated before we have any hope of dealing with the sexuality aspect of HIV/AIDS.

The redeemed humanity or 'Messiah humanity' actually returns to God's original intention for the race, including its sexuality. As the Bible has it, the original sex-related command to humanity (men and women equally) was, 'Be fruitful and multiply' (Genesis 1.28). Instead of this, many cultural patterns seem to assume that the first sex-related command was given to men only, 'Be dominant and enjoy yourself.' The contrast between these two views of the meaning of sex needs to be articulated in everyday language to every Christian on the planet as possibly the most important piece of 'sex education' they will ever receive.[6]

A positive yet disciplined theology of sexuality and a social space in which that theology can be discussed and assimilated among peers are two crucial features of the churches' contribution to the HIV/AIDS battle. While not wanting to point to any one simple solution as the answer to the crisis, we suspect that this twin contribution of the churches lies very close to the heart of the matter. It is simple at one level yet enormously complex to unpack and deliver. As that delivery occurs, a great deal of the latent capacity of the churches will be activated. Stigma will plummet. Abstinence and faithfulness campaigns will be much more effective because their theological framework will be clearer to the ordinary person and compliance will no longer rest on sheer obedience to church authority. More volunteers will step forward to fight alongside those described in this project . . .

Challenge: connections with secular groups, including governments

The challenge of connecting with secular groups[7] looms large in the minds of congregations in our survey. They know they need it, many are experimenting with it, but they also have some reservations about it and in some cases are almost resigned to it being an insoluble problem. Let us survey the scene and consider some possible ways around the main obstacles to effective collaboration with secular groups.

---

6 Besides the general theology of sexuality, many practical implications will need to be spelled out. For example, see the call of Zimbabwe for a 'theology of condom use'. Imagine that as a final exam question in a seminary classroom!

7 In this section, our survey deals primarily with the policies of the large donors, NGOs and governments, not much with practices of local NGOs or local government offices. The role of the smaller groups was a significant missing piece in our original research design and the problem was recognized too late to rectify. These small groups were mentioned in passing in several reports, but not with enough detail for our purposes.

The need for connections

All across the spectrum of countries in our sample, congregations acknowledge their need for assistance from governmental and other secular bodies. An email from Peru states: 'In the case of Peru it is the secular and government programs that have a lot to offer once the evangelical churches decide to work hard on prevention.' The country report from Zimbabwe describes the secular programmes as 'better focused', 'better trained and resourced', and 'providing more professional counseling' than the Christian volunteer programmes. The superior medical knowledge of the secular groups is acknowledged too in an email from Kenya:

> Similar transformation [from near death to apparent nearly full health] can take place when TB is first treated in a PLHA because TB mimics terminal AIDS. It is a sad fact that many people in Kenya (and quite likely elsewhere in Africa) thought to be dying of terminal AIDS in fact die of TB which has not been diagnosed or treated. In Kenya at least TB testing and treatment is free and available . . . For the Church to care properly there needs to be a basis of knowledge of the [medical] conditions, and what is available from government and other networks, and for the congregation to know how to access them.

Congregations need secular connections, and the reverse is also true at some points. For example, governments or secular NGOs may need supplementary support from a congregation or a faith-based organization in order to get their aid within actual reach of PLHA. An email from Kenya states:

> Even if the NGOs provide free treatment, the cost of getting to that treatment is prohibitive . . . At least one of the SPILL base groups provides the bus fares so that free treatment can be accessed. In saying this I want to emphasize the vital need to network with the other operators in the field. This is something the ordinary congregation can do, if they look outside the confines of their own congregation.

Current working connections

As a general trend, secular groups seem to be less closed to co-operation with Christian groups than previously,[8] and some are actively cultivating connections. Some high-level indications of this are found in Zambia and Nigeria. In June 2003, the Minister of Health of Zambia appointed the Zambian group in our study [ECR: see below] to a three-year term representing Zambian churches on the 15-member board of the National AIDS Council. The most optimistic reading of the state of play came from the Nigerian country report:

> Over time, secular organizations have come to accept that churches have a major role to play in the anti-HIV/AIDS campaign. Every effort is usually made to involve faith-based organizations at various levels of the campaign. For example, . . . the National Action Committee on AIDS . . . sponsored a faith-based initiative forum [in April 2004] to encourage religious leaders to play more prominent roles.

This view was supported by examples such as public praise by the National Action Committee on AIDS for the HIV/AIDS programme at a hospital run by the Redeemed Christian Church of God in the capital of Nigeria. The wide range of types of connections with secular groups in Nigeria is sketched in the following excerpt from the country report:[9]

Funded by secular organizations
Like other groups, church-based programmes are sponsored by secular/government, local and international organizations.

---

8 In 2003, Edward C. Green commented on the pattern of this lack of co-operation as follows: 'In general, [faith-based organizations] have received relatively little international support for either their care and treatment work or for their prevention activities.' He proposed, 'Steps should be taken to overcome any conflict or antagonism between a faith-based approach and a secular, public health approach.' See his September 2003 paper, 'Faith-Based Organizations: Contributions to HIV Prevention', USAID, pp. 6, 17.

9 The range of connections reported was broader in Nigeria than in the other countries, perhaps simply because of its size. Nigeria is more populous than all the other countries in the survey combined, excluding India, of course.

A number of programmes by the Catholic Church of Nigeria, Redeemed Christian Church of God, Baptist Convention of Nigeria and the Salvation Army are supported by Family Health International and funded by the United States Agency for International Development, the National Action Committee on AIDS (NACA) through the World Bank and Futures Groups International. Most of the funded programmes are production of IEC materials and organizing workshops, seminars and other awareness programmes.

Participation in conferences and workshops
Another point of connection between church-based programmes and secular groups is that officials of church-based programmes are sponsored to participate in local and international workshops.

Membership of coalitions and networks
There are a number of coalitions on some aspects of the HIV Campaigns like Access to Treatment, Network of People Living with HIV, and National, State and Local Action committees on HIV/AIDS, which officials of church HIV programmes belong to. Through the networks and coalitions, the church officials are able to influence policy issues and push for Christian perspectives to the campaign . . .

Table 9.1 shows the services that secular and Christian groups both offer and those offered only by the Christian groups, whether congregational or other.

The 'Uniquely Christian agenda' in the table revolves around an alternative 'big picture' of life. That 'big picture' provides a unique perspective on and approach to the struggle with HIV/AIDS. If we grasp this idea of the connection between that big picture of the Christian message and the work of Christians against HIV/AIDS, we will recognize that the distinction between the two sections of the table may be somewhat misleading. The lower section ('Uniquely Christian agenda') is not merely an additional list of items for Christians to work on: it is an additional dimension that provides a different context and a different internal power for Christians as they do all the things in

Table 9.1: Christian and secular agendas in the HIV/AIDS battle

Agents	Before	During	After
Shared Christian and secular agenda.	De-stigmatize. Raise awareness.	Promote voluntary counselling and testing. Promote 'living positively'. Provide tangibles (food, medicine, labour, etc.). Provide intangibles (group acceptance and valuation, counselling, encouragement, assurance that children will be cared for, etc.).	Foster care. Provide tangibles (food, labour, job training, etc.). Provide intangibles (group acceptance and valuation, counselling, encouragement, etc.).
Uniquely Christian agenda.	Develop Christian youth and marriages.	Bring confidence of salvation now and after death.	Lead to a life of joy and victory, directed by and filled with Jesus and the Holy Spirit.

the upper section (the same things that secular service agencies do).

As our report has shown, congregations are addressing the whole gamut of challenges in both sections of Table 9.1. Though their motivation for involvement is based on a different big picture than the secular one, their objectives and actions overlap to a very considerable degree with those of secular agencies. They are an ally of the secular agencies concerning the secular goals, and they supplement these with goals of their own . . .

Overcoming obstacles to partnership with secular approaches

Conflicting strategies are most apparent in the prevention phase of the HIV/AIDS battle. The debate about condoms and abstinence is a frequent flashpoint in discussions between Christian and secular AIDS workers, such as in the recent sharp debate about how much the government condom campaign and the church abstinence campaign each contributed to the drastic drop in HIV-positive rate in Uganda. Our survey asked what the differences are between help from Christians and help from government or non-religious groups. A Honduran focus group member stated a black-and-white answer that secular groups have heard from Christians for a long time: 'The government promotes the use of condoms; the Church promotes faithfulness (to the Lord and within the marriage relationship) and abstention.'

In countries that have been dealing with the crisis for a long time, the attitude toward condom usage is now becoming more nuanced. A Zambian focus group cautions, 'Churches should not "just" criticize anyhow those distributing condoms without being well informed of why, in what context, how, to whom, etc. But they should continue doing more in what they believe as a church is the best way to reduce infections.' The country report from Kenya warns, 'Churches must be careful not to defame the condom with false reports. When there is a fire in the house you use every method available to put it out.' The country report from Zimbabwe goes even further: 'The "theology" of condom use needs to be clearly propounded so that local churches can approach the subject in an objective way that is consistent with Christian values.' Perspectives like these open the way for much more exploration of the issue, including some common ground with some parts of the secular campaigns as well as some room for new development of Christian teaching.

Mismatched structures affect particularly the resourcing of congregational work in the phases of care for the infected and mitigation of impact on the affected. The structural mismatch is essentially between the formal, large-scale secular organizations and the informal, small-scale organization of the congregations. The Zimbabwe report says that the vast majority of churches tend to integrate HIV/AIDS ministry into all their existing activities such as worship, youth groups, Bible study groups, etc., rather than to set up an 'HIV/AIDS ministry' as a separate track within the congregation (though the latter is becoming more common). The informal approach may indeed be a highly effective way for churches to use their social and moral capital within their church communities to exert leverage for behavioural change; but even if it is, national governments and major secular donors will find it difficult or impossible to give money directly to church congregations to fund their programmes. The governments want groups to register as non-profits, but this requires a formal name, appointment of officers, holding a bank account that will be inspected, and the like. This is quite unrealistic for many of the very useful HIV/AIDS programmes that congregations are running. The governments and other secular donors need a middleman for their relationships with congregational programmes.

Two of the researchers in our survey, Bishop Joshua Banda (Zambia) and John Downing (Kenya), are themselves heavily invested in nationwide programmes that have potential as middlemen. Their structures integrate local Christians and congregations with a much larger network of resources, and they believe their models are replicable in other countries. The Zambian network is called ECR (Expanded Church Response). 'Expanded' refers to expanding denominational HIV/AIDS ministry by delivering it through all the local congregations that are affiliated. ECR is receiving grants from several secular groups. The principles of this inter-denominational network model are:

- local congregations are the key to winning the HIV/AIDS battle;
- the work of the congregations can be enhanced by a central office that co-ordinates, equips and resources the congregations;
- the central office engages in advocacy, grant negotiation, facilitation and sub-granting;
- the central office connects a broad spectrum of denominations that are willing to work together.

The Kenyan programme SPILL operates under the auspices of an interdenominational seminary, St Paul's United Theological College, Limuru. It is a unique masters programme for HIV/AIDS ministry leaders, which also mobilizes over 1,000 grass-roots volunteers, mostly from local congregations. Theoretically this might be an acceptable 'middleman' structure for secular donors, though it has not yet received significant amounts of secular funding. This training and mobilization model revolves around the following principles:

- grass-roots volunteers are the key to winning the HIV/AIDS battle;
- it is counter-productive to fund grass-roots volunteers to deliver AIDS services but urgent to find ways to enable them to provide material aid such as food, soap and medicine;
- it is very strategic to provide training and encouragement for grass-roots volunteers in clusters of 20 to 25.

Such training and encouragement does require some external funding for the cluster leaders, which can be effectively structured for an initial two to three years as part of a masters degree programme for HIV/AIDS ministry professionals.

What Christians and secular groups have learned about prevention

The experience of Christian churches and the secular groups in fighting HIV/AIDS is causing them to lose confidence in a basic assumption each had made about behaviour change. Many Christians assumed that preaching and moralizing about HIV/AIDS by church authorities would solve the problem. Many secular groups assumed that better information about HIV/AIDS would do the job. Millions are now dying of AIDS because of these theories, and the theories are dying a slow death with them.

Philosophically, both of those wrong assumptions rested on Enlightenment optimism, i.e. society's ills can be diagnosed by scholars, such as theologians, and solutions can be imposed by institutions, such as churches, that hold power over their members; and since human beings are basically rational beings, they will do what is reasonable if they have adequate information. Without venturing too far out toward the cynical end of postmodern thought, we may say, on the basis of HIV/AIDS statistics and trends, that the powers of institutional control and human rationality have been over-rated. Churches and secular bodies need to replace their demonstrably flawed assumptions in these areas with some more reliable ones.

This is not to say we should abandon all preaching and all AIDS awareness campaigns, but only that we all get over our assumptions about any quick fix or single-factor solution. What is needed is a multi-frontal attack on HIV/AIDS globally, the kind of attack that is typical of the few examples we have of success at a national level, such as Uganda, Senegal and Jamaica. We are not aware of any examples of success, in or beyond our survey, where the government and the religious bodies did not collaborate. Let neither side go it alone, taking pot-shots at the flawed assumption of the other without recognizing the flaws in its own assumption, as explained above. The two sides need each other like blades of a scissors or wings of a bird. If they refuse to co-ordinate their effort, a lot of it will be wasted.

Therefore, Christian congregations must more effectively provide what they are specially or even uniquely positioned to contribute, and they must also cultivate better connections with Christian and secular groups that work at national or international levels. In what follows, I will describe those two tasks as complementary. Success in either one makes success easier in the other.

The church contribution vis-à-vis the secular one

As we have noted in Table 9.1, there is very considerable overlap between Christian and secular goals and also significant ways in which Christian approaches go beyond the secular ones. Congregations are often picking up where the secular programmes leave off. For example:

1 Secular agencies can and do promote communal acceptance of PLHA, which is excellent, but they have to do it without mentioning the cross of Christ and the presence of the Holy Spirit. This severely handicaps their best efforts to confront deeply embedded cultural patterns such as how shame is generated and handled.

2 Secular agencies can communicate that there is life after AIDS, that various techniques of living with the disease can greatly enhance and extend life. Thank God for every new breakthrough they discover and teach. But they cannot supplement this with any clear equivalent to Christian participation in God's mission during this life or any hope to hold out for the afterlife.

3 The secular activists are at a distinct disadvantage when it comes to mobilizing and motivating volunteers. In a world that assumes economic and national self-interest to be everyone's guiding light, altruism is difficult to nurture. There are occasional (and in my view, ghastly) attempts to make the non-altruistic argument that the North should take an interest in HIV/AIDS in the South because the depopulation of Africa would be bad for business. But is anyone listening?

Some may note that the response to the recent tsunami in south Asia seems to indicate that people can still be moved by altruism and compassion to alleviate suffering, but this only proves that these forces can work as knee-jerk reactions. Our point is that there is no comparable reaction when the disaster unfolds over 20 years instead of 20 seconds. A 20-year response requires an intellectual and moral base, neither an emotional one nor one constantly propped up by televized news. Our claim is that the churches have that base, found in their central mission of representing the Messiah to the community.

4 Secular agencies can move some Northerners toward compassion for HIV/AIDS sufferers – and thank God for every one they do – but churches are much better positioned to move Northerners toward identification with the Southern Christian volunteers serving those who suffer. For example, churches in the North are sending tens of thousands of volunteers overseas every year on short-term 'mission trips'

of one to two weeks. The direct contribution of these to the HIV crisis may be small, but the face-to-face connections with local Christians, such as those fostering AIDS orphans, can lead to long-term international connections that bear fruit over a lifetime.

In the above examples we have been pointing out various aspects of what appears to us to be Christian supplements that make up for secular deficiencies. Nevertheless, we do not wish to imply that the churches have all the answers and the world has everything wrong. Far from it. The enemy is HIV/AIDS, not secularists. The problem Christians have with secular (and many traditional) ideas is often that they simply do not go far enough in the right direction they are headed; they do not provide what it takes to reach their desired goals. Christianity provides the missing power in the person of the Holy Spirit, who connects people to the life-giving power of the Messiah today.

We hasten to add that we are not given the power so that we can lord it over anyone else. We are sent out as servants, carrying the message that the power is available to anyone else who wants to have it on Jesus' terms. And whether people accept that message or not, the life-giving Spirit still guides us to work with any and all who are in the business of promoting life.

We therefore believe that there is a very promising future in closer partnerships between congregations, other faith-based organizations and secular organizations along the lines outlined above. Forging those partnerships becomes easier as all sides become more aware of each other's perspectives, even when those perspectives are not held in common.

10. The Yale Divinity School Women's Initiative on AIDS

MARGARET A. FARLEY

Undertaking the Women's Initiative at Yale Divinity School . . . would allow us to respond to the AIDS pandemic precisely as theologians. Here was a project for which our training and capabilities specifically as theologians and ethicists could be genuinely useful, indeed central. We had gradually become convinced that religious traditions have been both a part of the problem regarding the spread of the HIV infection and a part of the remedy. We recognized that if religious traditions have anything at all to say to situations such as the HIV/AIDS crisis, they must speak about God (or whatever is for them ultimate) and about our responsibilities to one another in relation to God. They must speak, then, about the possibilities of hope for those whose hope is threatened or shattered in the face of disease and death. Moreover, if religious traditions have anything to say that is a healing word, a strengthening and promising word, in such situations, it must be a word that is embodied in deeds. Short of this, religious traditions will be, as they have all too often been in relation to the spread of HIV, more a part of the problem than a part of any remedy. The first response of most people who stand in religious traditions and have any understanding at all of the AIDS pandemic is compassion. But 'compassion' can be an empty word unless there is a clear-sighted recognition of what compassion requires.

All major world religions have had something to say in response to the large questions of people's lives, including the question of suffering. Far from being completely irrational, religions have helped to make sense of parts of life in relation to wholes, of aspects of life that philosophy alone has not been able to fathom. In so doing, they have given meaning to both the ordinary and extraordinary experiences of people, and they have shed light on our responsibilities to one another. In the Yale Divinity School Women's Initiative our questions became: What does all of this mean in the context of the suffering and potential suffering surrounding HIV/AIDS in sub-Saharan Africa? What is required of faith communities, for example, as interpreters of the pandemic and as transformers of some of its causes? Every kind of care is needed – for prevention, treatment and ongoing support of all who are affected by the pandemic. Care is needed in ways that religious groups and institutions can give and in ways they cannot by themselves provide. Religious caregivers can organize clinics, reach out to rural areas, advocate for desperately needed medicines, personnel and equipment, raise prophetic voices in calling the world to respond. But faith communities must also critically review their role in shaping beliefs, constructing attitudes and reinforcing behaviours that have contributed to the spread of AIDS. Just as religious traditions are profoundly influenced by the cultures in which they are embedded, so cultures are shaped and reinforced by the religions that are a part of them.

Take, for example, the response by churches, mosques and temples to issues of sexuality as they are relevant to the spread of HIV infection. Though there are now some signs of change in this regard, silence has generally surrounded these issues. Cultural expectations, frequently informed by and reinforced by religion, make questions of sexual behaviour, marital fidelity, sexual orientation and prostitution highly sensitive questions. Behind the silence lies, to some extent, a concern for privacy, perhaps even a belief that everyone knows the answers to such questions. Yet, in a deeper sense, the silence represents profound fear and shame, and a tendency to the self-protection of families and communities that is the result of shame at an individual member's breaking of perceived taboos. This shame can result even if the taboos are customarily broken, as in the tacit acceptance of married men's need for prostitutes as partners when they must travel away from home in order to secure employment.

When it comes to HIV, a whole chain of stigmatization may be falsely imposed on individuals (as in blaming wives for their husbands' infection); and it is not a simple matter to change the focus of stigma in the public mind.

Sometimes the response within religious traditions is simply to reiterate moral rules which prohibit behaviours that happen also to put persons at risk of infection. Such a response has often not been very successful. Indeed, it has all too often heightened the shame and the stigma associated with AIDS, and it has prevented behavioural changes that might actually be remedies against the disease, such as the use of condoms and the achievement of greater freedom of choice on the part of women. Religious traditions do not hesitate to rethink their moral rules in other spheres of human life – social, political, economic spheres – when situations demand it. All too often, however, a taboo morality (bolstered by both religion and culture) holds sway in the sexual sphere, a morality whose power depends on resisting critical examination, thus preventing the transformation of traditional beliefs as well as practices.

Similarly, the problems that follow from gender bias are problems not foreign to religious traditions. In fact, there is a particular claim on faith communities that has not yet fully been met. The United Nations may declare international years of women, and particular countries may introduce measures to protect women from abuse and to assist them with their children. The new African Union may articulate women's rights that must be respected and secured.[1] But if faith traditions do not address the gender bias that remains deep in their own teachings and practices, changes for women may come too late to protect them from AIDS. This surely is the time for those who stand in religious traditions to press the question of the role of patriarchal religions in making women invisible, subordinate, passive in the face of what destroys them.

---

1 As of 14 July 2003, the text of the new African Union proposed treaty on women's human rights was available online at http://www.hrea.org/erc/Library/display.php?doc_id=806&category_id=31. It must be noted, however, that by the end of 2003 the member nations had not yet signed the treaty.

One more consideration must be taken into account here. The work that we were undertaking in the Yale Divinity School Women's Initiative would be cross-cultural as well as interfaith work. In so far as faith communities in Africa must critically review their role in shaping beliefs, attitudes and behaviours relevant to HIV/AIDS, how could our own work as primarily North American theologians and ethicists be useful to this task? Sensitive to the ongoing temptations to intellectually colonize peoples in other parts of the world, but also reminded by our friends in the Circle of Concerned African Women Theologians that our role could not be simply that of passive listeners, we took seriously the fact that we are co-believers in shared religious traditions. The traditions with which our project would be concerned are by and large traditions of world religions.[2] Hence, the questions raised of these traditions in the context of HIV/AIDS, even in Africa, are questions for us all. Within Christianity in particular, the time has come when the concept of 'world church' may finally be given content. No longer is the issue primarily the 'inculturation' of this faith and its practices throughout the world. Rather, to understand Christianity as a 'world church' is to recognize that the Christian gospel is not meant to be only or even primarily a Western European or North American gospel, exported, like the rest of Western culture, to other parts of the world. God's self-revelation can be not only received but also given in every language. Out of every language and culture it can be spoken as well as heard. No single culturally influenced interpretation can therefore exercise total control over its forms. Yet, many of the problematic aspects of Christian teachings (as well as those of other world

---

2 Clearly the influence of local religions is extremely important in African contexts where HIV/AIDS is rampant. We were not unconcerned about these. But our primary engagement would be with world religious traditions – Christianity, Islam, Judaism and to some extent Hinduism and Buddhism. Women from these traditions would be the ones who would first engage with us in partnership, and they are the ones who are struggling with the responses of their traditions to the AIDS pandemic. Clearly, also, given our primarily Christian backgrounds, the task of reviewing the Christian tradition would be central to what we could do, at least in the beginnings of the project.

religions) regarding, for example, sexuality, gender relations, family structure, and institutional roles, have been exported by a Western Church around the world. In so far as any of these exported teachings have contributed to the stigma surrounding AIDS, the constraints on women in responding to AIDS, and the obstacles to preventing HIV/AIDS, they require critique and reconstruction – a task for us all.

All of these considerations provided impetus for the formation of the Yale Divinity School Women's Initiative in response to HIV/AIDS in Africa. We were clear from the start, however, that such a project would have to be shaped according to certain norms – norms that would incorporate feminist and [black] womanist commitments, respect for cultures different from the one dominant at Yale Divinity School, and the establishment of partnerships without which our work would be in vain.

Normative shaping of a response to HIV/AIDS in Africa

From the start, all of us from Yale Divinity School who became involved in the Women's Initiative knew that we needed one another to take on the tasks before us. Among ourselves, the most important thing we shared was our mutual commitment to the goals of the project. No one of us would have undertaken a project like this alone. In addition, we had within our small group (grown to 12) significant resources for interdisciplinary work. Our fields included theology, ethics, pastoral counselling, multi-level education, women's studies, cross-cultural studies, biblical studies, pastoral ministry, organization and management. We came from a variety of Christian denominations: Baptist, Disciples of Christ, Episcopal, Methodist, Presbyterian, Roman Catholic, United Church of Christ. We represented different age groups and to some extent different cultures and countries: United States, Mexico, Cameroon, Kenya, Botswana.

Nonetheless, we could not by ourselves make much difference in response to the AIDS pandemic. It was clearly essential that we partner with persons whose experience was broader than ours; we needed funding; we needed expertise in working with worldwide HIV/AIDS; we needed colleagues from the cultural contexts which we hoped to address and support. We needed partnerships with Yale Divinity School, USAID/CORE and the Circle of Concerned African Women Theologians. Moreover, we were committed not only to a partnered construction of the project's agenda, but to yielding primary voice in the ongoing shaping and implementation of the agenda to those who would be most affected by it – that is, to our African partners. We gradually learned from them, however, not only to provide space for African women to speak with one another, but to share an active dialogue that would include us all who are committed to faith-grounded, life-affirming responses to HIV and AIDS. Its fourfold task would be to:

1 address the intersections of gender, faith and HIV/AIDS in ways that lead to the empowerment of women;
2 focus the theological resources of worldwide communities of faith in order to transform traditional beliefs and attitudes regarding sexuality and the status of women;
3 discern and articulate, in the context of international partnership, useful next steps (including the identification of financial resources) that can be taken in Africa regarding women's response to HIV/AIDS;
4 discover elements for future actions and potential networks whereby women theologians in the US can be in solidarity with and accountable to women of faith in Africa who are addressing HIV/AIDS; and whereby US women theologians can better address the challenges of HIV/AIDS in the US.

What came to be called the 'Consultation on Gender, Faith, and Responses to HIV/AIDS in Africa' took place during three days, 28 February to 3 March 2002. Fifty women from 16 countries and 14 different faith traditions gathered at Yale Divinity School to share their experiences of HIV/AIDS, and to engage in gender analysis, general social analysis, and theological reflection. Among the participants were 23 women from African nations such as Kenya and Ghana, and as far south as Zambia, Zimbabwe and South Africa. The majority of other participants were from the United States, but Mexico and Canada were also represented. In their many countries, the participants held (and hold) a variety of positions in the academy, pastoral ministry and HIV/AIDS care and prevention.

The programme of the consultation incorporated plenary sessions, smaller working groups, interfaith and ecumenical worship services, visits to local HIV/AIDS-related agencies and organizations, and action planning for the future. Plenary sessions were designed to:

1 share information about work already being done by African women in faith communities, responding to the AIDS pandemic;
2 identify, from diverse perspectives, theological and ethical imperatives for women, for churches, for believers who fill whatever roles in families and institutions;
3 invite storytelling, the sharing of poetry, music and art, as well as personal testimony regarding experiences of HIV/AIDS.

One plenary was opened to the wider public – to medical care-givers, local pastoral ministers and leaders in the struggle against AIDS. Out of this session, new partnerships began – in particular, between the Yale Divinity School Women's Initiative and the Center for Interdisciplinary Research on AIDS (CIRA – a centre lodged in Yale's Medical School, Department of Epidemiology and Public Health).

Working groups included internationally mixed groups addressing issues of sexuality, cultural practices, gender relationships, poverty, political instability, needs for medical care (as well as food, education, employment), interfaith alliances in response to HIV/AIDS, potential resources for the theoretical and practical work of women on all of these issues. There were also nationally focused working groups sharing and interpreting experiences of HIV/AIDS in their own contexts.

Finally, national and regional groups met to identify 'next steps' to be taken after the consultation. Among these were a commitment to support the August 2002 conference to be sponsored by the Circle (including a search for funding through

CORE/USAID as well as other sources); an expanded effort on the part of the Yale Divinity School Women's Initiative to involve other seminaries and divinity schools in similar responses to the AIDS pandemic, not only in Africa but in South and East Asia and in Latin America; the strengthening of partnerships already in place through the formation of a continuing accountability group (a steering committee) and the inauguration of an electronic newsletter; commitment to support of publications by African women theologians through a search for publishers and funding; and the establishment of HIV/AIDS training centres as part of existing theological centres in Africa. What has actually followed the consultation at Yale reflects these plans for action, though some of them remain in early stages. 'Life after the consultation' has been full, however, as the commitment – especially between members of the Yale Divinity School Women's Initiative and the Circle – unfolds.

Partnership in hope: the continuous and the new

One project spawns other projects; one task leads to another; one relationship opens to others. Why is this? I suppose there is, first of all, a relentless logic to it all. Awakening leads to colleagueship and commitment; modest forms of organization and community tend to stabilize responses; new possibilities and imperatives unfold. The logic is both intellectual and affective, personal and social, a logic of both obligation and, yes, love. The fruits of our consultation cannot be described in terms of dramatic successes, but they do represent a sustained bonding among persons and determination to resist the forces of death. Let me describe some of the developments that are a direct consequence of the partnerships that led to the consultation and the commitments that came at its end.

First, leaders of the Circle invited four members of the Yale Divinity School Women's Initiative to attend the Circle's August 2002 conference on 'Sex, Stigma and HIV/AIDS: African Women Challenging Religion, Culture, and Social Practices'. Held in Addis Ababa, Ethiopia, this was the third Pan-African Conference sponsored by the Circle for its members; it was the first to focus on HIV/AIDS; it was the first to invite a small number of non-African women (including the four from the Yale Divinity School Initiative) to join with its member-participants. Approximately 140 African women theologians from 25 African countries came together to address the HIV/AIDS pandemic.[3] All Circle participants brought papers prepared for the conference on issues of the role of faith communities in response to AIDS; theological resources that contribute to women's self-empowerment; sharing of resources; sex and sexuality; theological and ethical challenges of the AIDS crisis; socio-cultural practices that promote the spread of HIV; biblical and theological resources relevant to the AIDS crisis; and forms of support and solidarity for people living with HIV and AIDS. In and from the conference came a Circle response to HIV/AIDS – a response in accord with its mission to foster African women's theological research, writing and publishing on African issues from women's perspective; a response from the 'safe space' of the conference that carried the power of a new consolidation of efforts ('in all our areas of work'[4]) on the part of African women who are theologically trained. For those of us from the United States, the conference revealed and bore witness to the overall power of African women, the utter importance of African women's theology in the context of AIDS, the contours of a path going further into the heart of the AIDS pandemic, and the strength and hope needed to take this path.

In a closing session of the Circle conference, we from the YDS Women's Initiative were able to describe a second development, directly consequent upon our earlier collaboration with the Circle at the consultation at Yale. That is, we announced and sought applicants for a new Yale University Research Affiliate ('fellowship') Program in theology and public health. The partnership between Yale Divinity School and Yale's Department of Epidemiology and Public Health, which began after the open session of the February/March consultation, had by now

---

3 See Musimbi Kanyoro (ed.), *Report of the Third Pan African Conference of the Circle of Concerned African Women Theologians*, Addis Ababa, Ethiopia, 4–8 August 2002.

4 Isabel Apawo Phiri, 'Keynote Address', in Kanyoro, *Report*, p. 26.

led to a joint sponsorship of a research affiliation open specifically to African women theologians. This post-doctoral programme aims to combine theology, faith community initiatives and empirical research on HIV/AIDS prevention and care in Africa. It is essentially interdisciplinary, in that it must incorporate both theological research and empirical research (qualitative or quantitative).

The rationale behind this research affiliate programme is based on the premise that faith plays an important role in individual and community life and can influence social and health behaviour. Despite this fact, very little scholarly empirical research has been done to examine the actual or potential impact of faith-oriented prevention initiatives on the African continent. Recognizing the need for just this sort of research as part of public health initiatives, CIRA (in Yale's Department of Epidemiology and Public Health) mediated funds to make this joint programme possible. It is now two years in progress – having hosted three African women theologians in the spring of 2003, and two more for the academic year 2003–04. Recruitment and selection of candidates for this programme is done through the Circle. Each of these individuals has proposed and refined (with the addition of their theological studies and training in public health methodology at Yale) a research protocol, to be implemented in their own African countries. Members of the Yale Divinity School Women's Initiative serve as mentors to these affiliates, as do faculty from CIRA and the Department of EPH. The partnerships go on, both organizational and individual.

Individuals within the Yale Divinity School Women's Initiative are also involved in direct efforts to facilitate the publication of Circle members' books. This has involved collaborative (with the Circle) general support, editorial assistance and negotiation for subsidies so that the books can be published both in Africa (where they are more affordable to Africans) and in the West (where marketing and distribution are necessary if scholars outside Africa are be aware of them and interact with them in their cross-cultural work). The Circle itself has published more than thirty volumes since its inauguration, a sign that its commitment to foster African women's scholarship is being well kept. Yet there are more publications to be nurtured and facilitated to completion. This is one of the Yale Divinity School Women's Initiative's ways of being faithful to the partnerships it has undertaken.

Further, the Yale Divinity School Women's Initiative has been in communication – through colleagueship in the American Academy of Religion and the Society of Biblical Literature – with feminist and womanist scholars in universities, colleges and seminaries across the US. The aim of this communication has been to inspire other women religious scholars to consider projects similar or analogous to the one at Yale Divinity School – in relation to Africa, perhaps, but also to Asian and Latin American countries, and to our own country as well. The supposition is that networks with women theologians in these parts of the world can help to address the AIDS pandemic as it moves with rapid speed through the many other countries of the South, and as it continues to affect communities in the US itself.

Finally, a new project regarding women's responses to HIV/AIDS in Africa has developed out of the Yale Divinity School Women's Initiative. One of the difficulties we encountered in identifying African women theologians for our original consultation was finding African Roman Catholic women trained in theology. The Circle is, of course, interfaith, so that although the majority of its members are Protestant Christian, they do include Roman Catholic Christians as well as Muslims and Jews. Yet the Catholics are few; only a handful came to our attention through the whole of our efforts. In the end, the consultation had five Catholic participants. Speaking with them, and with other colleagues around the world, I explored the idea of a conference in Africa for Roman Catholic women – whether trained as theologians or not, as long as they had some knowledge of their faith tradition.

To make what has become a very long story (and a rich part of my own journey into the crisis of HIV/AIDS in Africa) as brief as possible here in this limited chapter, let me say only that I and a colleague of mine, Eileen Hogan, now co-direct a project called All Africa Conference: Sister to Sister (AACSS). We have worked hard to find African Catholic women theologians, with some success. We have, with them, sought the kind of network, expertise and partnership that has been possible with the Circle in relation to the Yale Divinity School Women's Initiative. The networks we found were in and among religious orders of women. Here are women trained at least to some extent in the riches as well as the challenges of their faith tradition, and here are women who are already working on the front lines of the AIDS pandemic. Not one, but three conferences are now part of this project – the first one having taken place in eastern Africa in August 2003. A second and a third are in the planning stages for southern and western Africa. The journey is as intense and complex an experience as has been the original and ongoing journey that began from Yale. Its goal is the same: effective responding to AIDS. Its way is the same: the mutual self-empowerment of women of faith, breaking the silence among themselves, identifying their own ways to respond to the AIDS pandemic.

Meaning of the past in the present, meaning of the present for the future

In the end, which of course is not an end but only a reflection *in medias res*, what can be said about this journey thus far? Some insights stand out: there is a shared responsibility for the dying that continues to threaten. Fourteen million are dead, and counting. The causes of the pandemic are complex and confusing. Yet it is clear that no one in our shrinking global community is without reasons to respond. Whether it is because we are all sisters and brothers in the human race, or because we share in religious traditions, or because we affirm solidarity among women across the globe, or because some of us and our countries or traditions are implicated in the oppressive conditions that fuel the pandemic: this is a situation from which it is difficult to justify our turning away.

Feminists and womanists have learned to respect other traditions, cultures, beliefs and convictions. It is not up to women in one part of the world to critique cultural practices that involve women in another part of the world. Yet when cultural practices harm women (and children and men), and when multitudes die of the practices, then if women – themselves in the cultures at stake – rise up to critique the practices, we can stand with them in solidarity. Just as Western women have critiqued our own culture and the role of religion within it, we should not be indifferent when other women offer critiques in their contexts, out of experiences of their own.

Womanists have taught feminists not to use the stories of some women to enhance the productivity of other women. This is a lesson none of us can forget. But partnerships can be formed around genuinely common tasks, to which everyone contributes and from which everyone may gain. Out of the experience of such partnerships come imperatives for all – imperatives to care for one another, and in doing so, to resist the forces of diminishment and death. It is possible to share journeys, marvellous and terrible, from which none of us can turn back.

11. Counselling AIDS Patients: Job as a Paradigm

GUNTHER H. WITTENBERG

The challenge of the AIDS pandemic has not yet been sufficiently realized by the Church. As the disease spreads and starts to disrupt communities it will increasingly become a dominant issue for ministers who take their calling as counsellors seriously.

The basic requirement for the counsellor of AIDS patients is the recognition that the illness involves three dimensions of suffering – the physical, the psychic and the social – which, taken together, characterize it as a major calamity. There is first of all the physical side, the illness itself, which for those tested HIV-positive will perhaps not be immediately apparent but which will become more important as the virus breaks down the immune system of the patient. The illness also puts great demands on the mental and spiritual resources of the patient who needs to cope with the awareness that there is no cure for the illness, that death is its sure goal. The third dimension of suffering is social, the problem of rejection by family and friends, perhaps loss of job and ostracism in society. A recognition that AIDS patients are hurting in all three dimensions is a precondition for any deeper understanding of its problems.[1]

What is the goal of counselling in such a situation? The counsellor needs to mobilize the spiritual resources to enable the

---

1 On the three dimensions of suffering, see Dorothea Sölle, 1973, *Leiden*, Stuttgart: Kreux (English translation: 1975, *Suffering*, Philadelphia: Fortress).

patient to cope with the physical pain, to understand himself or herself and the suffering, and to be liberated from social isolation in an atmosphere of acceptance.

One of the most important tools of the Christian counsellor is the Bible. It tells the story of people in many different situations of suffering and their experiences with God. It thus offers paradigms with which patients today can identify. By re-telling biblical stories the counsellor helps the patients to reorient themselves in the light of the experiences of the people of the Bible and to enable them to understand themselves in their own anguish and to cope with their situation. In this sense the Bible can develop its truly liberatory potential. But there is also another side of which the counsellor has to be aware. Religious language does not only liberate and lead to new perspectives and change, but it can also increase the agony of the patient when it offers religious 'solutions' to the problems of suffering which do not help but rather confine the sufferer to his or her own isolation. Used in this way the Bible no longer liberates but becomes repressive.[2]

A particularly valuable example of this ambivalent nature of religious language and therefore all counselling is the story of Job and how he had to cope with a situation of extreme suffering involving all three dimensions – the physical pain, the psychic agony and the social ostracism. Its significance for the counsellor of AIDS patients lies in the fact that it demonstrates how talking about God can aggravate the misery instead of leading to a productive transformation and acceptance of suffering on the part of the patient. The story of Job can therefore serve as a true paradigm both for the counsellor and for the suffering person. It teaches both how not to talk about God and also how to talk *to* God. In the following, I explore both these aspects and draw some conclusions out of this discussion for the counselling of AIDS patients.

---

2 See Ulrich Eibach, 1991, 'Der Leidende Mensch vor Gott. Krankheit und Behinderung als Heraus-forderung unseres Bildes von Gott und dem Mensehen Theologie in Seelsorge, Beratung und Diakonia 2', Neukirchen-Vlutn: Neukirehener, p. 18.

How not to talk about God – Job's friends as counsellors

Chapters 1 and 2 of the book of Job tell how the wealthy farmer Job is struck by one misfortune after the other. First he loses all his possessions and also his children, and finally he is inflicted by a painful and loathsome skin disease. According to Old Testament scholars this story was a popular narrative which was used by the author of the book as a framework for the discussion of the problem of suffering which begins in chapter 3. The final sentences of the narrative section set the stage: 'Now when Job's three friends heard of all these troubles that had come upon him, each of them set out from his home Eiphaz the Temanite, Bildad the Shuhite, and Zophar the Naamathite. They met together to go and console and comfort him' (Job 2.11). The purpose of their visit was therefore to support Job in his troubles.

Before they even started to talk, they 'raised their voices and wept aloud', they tore their clothes and then they were silent for seven days and nights as a sign of solidarity and compassion with Job, because 'they saw that his suffering was very great' (2.13). Only when Job, in an outburst of despair, gave vent to his great grief and cursed the day of his birth, did his friends begin to counsel him. The purpose of this 'counselling' was to comfort and support Job, but it developed more and more into a heated dispute about the nature and meaning of his suffering.

Both Job and his friends ask the question: 'Why?' Why did such a great calamity befall a man who was a wealthy and respected citizen of the community? For Job's friends the answer was obvious: Job's illness was a punishment for his sins.

At the background of this interpretation stands the conception of a perfect and just universe in which every human deed is followed by its consequences. Good deeds are followed by good consequences, evil deeds by evil consequences.[3] The person who obeys God's will and lives a just and righteous life will be

---

3 See Klaus Koch, 1983, 'Is There a Doctrine of Retribution in the Old Testament?' in James L. Crenshaw (ed.), *Theodicy in the Old Testament: Issues in Religion and Theology* 4, Philadelphia: Fortress, pp. 57–87.

blessed with prosperity, a large family and happiness. On the other hand, the wicked person who transgresses God's commandments will encounter misfortune and disaster. As in nature the seed develops into plants and fruit, so in God's just and moral universe good and evil deeds are followed almost automatically by their respective consequences, reward or punishment (cf. Proverbs 14.22, 22.8; Hosea 8.7, 10.13; Job 15.35; Psalms 7.15; Isaiah 59.4).

Because both deed and consequence are insolubly linked, the same Hebrew terms are used for the 'evil deed' or 'crime' and the resulting 'misfortune', for the 'sin' or 'trespass' and the 'punishment' which follows it.[4] 'Misfortune' and 'punishment' are but a logical and inevitable consequence of the evil deed (cf. Proverbs 11.30, 12.21). According to this theory every person is himself responsible for his fate. What he sows he will reap, be it good or bad. The violent will encounter violence (Psalms 7.16), and he who 'clothed himself with cursing' will experience that the curses will 'soak into his body like water' (Psalms 109.17–19).

We cannot deny that this conception gives expression to a basic human need. The wish that those who do good should also have a good life and those who do evil should receive their just punishment agrees with the basic human desire for justice. God's justice is seen in the guarantee of a moral universe.[5] The statement that punishment and suffering are the consequence of evil actions can often be supported by experience. The problem only arises when the statement is reversed. The fact that a person is visited by misfortune or illness is now taken as an indication that he or she must have committed a crime. The greater the misfortune, the greater the crime.[6] Job's friends are there-

---

4 Erhard Gerstenberger and Wolfgang Schrage, 1977, *Leiden*, Köhlhammer Taschenbücher Biblische Konfrontationen 1004, Stuttgart: Köhlhammer, p. 91; Ernst Kutsch, 1986, 'Von Grund und Sinn des Leidens nach dem Alten Testament' in Ernst Kutsch, *Kieine Schriften zum Alten Testament* BZAW 168, Berlin: Walter de Gruyter, p. 339.

5 See Eibach, 'Der Leidende Mensch', p. 33.

6 In the Old Testament there is a development of this conception to the rigidity of a dogma. This can be seen by comparing 2 Kings 15.5 with 2 Chronicles 26.20–21. King Azariah (Uzziah) of Judah was struck with

fore certain that Job must have sinned.[7] Eliphaz enunciates the principle:

> Think now, who that was innocent ever perished?
> Or where were the upright cut off?
> As I have seen, those who plough iniquity
> and sow trouble reap the same.
> By the breath of God they perish,
> and by the blast of his anger they are consumed. (Job 4.7–8)

Bildad underscores this view with a reference to the wisdom of the fathers. They have found that there is no misfortune without transgression.

> For inquire now of bygone generations,
> and consider what their ancestors have found.
> Will they not teach you and tell you
> and utter words out of their understanding?
> Can papyrus grow where there is no marsh?
> Can reeds flourish where there is no water?
> While yet in flower and not cut down,
> they wither before any other plant.
> Such are the paths of all who forget God;
> the hope of the godless shall perish. (Job 8.8–13)

The friends urge Job to accept this position.

> See, we have searched this out; it is true.
> Hear, and know it for yourself. (Job 5.27)

Because they are sure that Job's illness is caused by his sin, they 'counsel' him to repent and to submit himself to God's judgement. Eliphas says:

---

leprosy by Yahweh. The author of Chronicles concludes that he must have committed a sin. This is supplied in verses 16–19. Uzziah made an offering which was restricted only to the priests. He became leprous as a punishment (see Kutsch, *Kieine Schriften*, p. 339).

7 See Gustavo Gutierrez, 1991, *On Job: God-talk and the Suffering of the Innocent*, Maryknoll, NY: Orbis, p. 21.

> As for me, I would seek God,
> and to God I would commit my cause. (Job 5.8)

God reproves and disciplines, he inflicts punishment, but he also delivers from troubles when there is true repentance (Job 5.17–26). Because God 'knows those who are worthless' and punishes iniquity (Job 11.11, 12), it is time for Job to 'put it far away' (v. 14).

> Surely then you will lift up your face without blemish;
> you will be secure, and will not fear.
> You will forget your misery. (Job 11.15–16)

Eliphas, Bildad and Sophar are competent theologians. They are convinced that their doctrine can explain Job's case. But Job denies that he is guilty. He does not deny that he is a sinner, as all human beings are sinners. His contention is that there is no reason why he should have earned this punishment. There was nothing in his life which should have merited such extreme suffering:

> Teach me, and I will be silent;
> make me understand how I have gone wrong. (Job 6.24)

Job's refusal to accept their interpretation now leads to increasing confrontation. Instead of counselling Job, his friends defend God's justice. They use all the arguments which have been used by theologians through the ages to defend God and to explain the suffering in this world. 'Even if you have not committed serious crimes, you have sinned because you do not fear God. You defy him and his wisdom' (Job 15). 'Surely, you must belong to the wicked. Your anger is an indication that there is something wrong with you' (Job 18). 'All experience teaches that the pride with which you try to mount to heaven to challenge God, will soon come to naught' (Job 20). 'Don't be so stubborn. Submit to God, accept his instruction and you will be at peace' (Job 22.21). 'Use the possibilities of prayer and worship to be reconciled to God, then things will be better' (Job 33).[8] In chapter 32, Elihu

---

8 Gerstenberger and Schrage, *Leiden*, p. 67.

the Buzite, who is introduced rather abruptly by the author, uses a new argument to defend God. It no longer focuses on the origin of Job's suffering, but on the purpose. God inflicts pain in order to educate and bring humans to insight. Suffering is a means of God's pedagogy.

> God indeed does all these things,
> twice, three times, with mortals,
> to bring back their soul from the Pit,
> so that they may see the light of life. (Job 33.29, 30).

Job rejects all these arguments. He rejects a theology which places the responsibility for all the suffering of the world on the suffering persons themselves in order to clear God of all blame. The logic of this theology is indisputable. 'The Almighty will not pervert justice' (Job 34.12) and 'How can a mortal be righteous before God?' These are truths which seem to be self-evident to Job's friends. God is almighty and just. He will inflict pain only in accordance with this justice. Indeed, this doctrine is very handy for explaining the suffering of others. But to Job, in the situation of his suffering, it has lost all meaning. These statements trap him in the logic of a system, without offering him any real help in his own distress. Instead, this theology becomes a theology of repression hiding its cruelty against the suffering of others in the pious garb of theological language purporting to defend God. How devoid of truth the theology of Job's friends had become in the course of the dispute becomes apparent in the sadistic wish of Elihu:

> Would that Job were tried to the limit,
> because his answers are those of the wicked. (Job 34.36)

With this, Job's isolation is complete. Forsaken by family (his wife, chapter 2) and friends, and punished and rejected by God, he is left to himself. The theological 'counselling' of his 'friends', their talk about God, is without any meaning. It would be better for them to remain silent (Job 13.5) than to 'whitewash with lies' all the injustices and suffering in this world (Job 13.4). By uttering 'windy words' they have become 'miserable comforters' (Job 16.2, 3) and 'worthless physicians' (Job 13.4).

How to talk to God – Job's protest and lament

For an understanding of the book of Job, Job 16.2–6 is a key text.[9] In order to become relevant for the situation of suffering, theologians cannot be 'miserable comforters'. Job rejects a theology which starts with abstract theological concepts but ignores the concrete life situation, suffering and hope of human beings. What Job's friends are saying is predictable. They utter abstract theological 'truths' which have no link with real life because they have never experienced Job's pain. Job criticizes theology which has lost contact with reality and does not display any solidarity with those who suffer.

Job's experience highlights the glaring discrepancy between what one would expect according to the doctrine of just reward and punishment, and the actual situation of the world. If, according to God's justice, the righteous should receive prosperity and happiness and the wicked punishment,

> Why do the wicked live on,
> reach old age, and grow mighty in power?
> Their children are established in their presence, and their
>   offspring before their eyes.
> Their houses are safe from fear,
> and no rod of God is upon them.
> They spend their days in prosperity,
> and in peace they go down to Sheol. (Job 21.7–9, 13)

The wicked 'remove landmarks', seize the flocks of the poor, oppress and exploit them (see chapter 24), but do not receive their just reward. Instead, God prolongs their life and gives them security (24.22–23). On the other hand, it is often the innocent, those who have done nothing wrong, who are oppressed, who suffer hardships, who are plagued by illness and have to endure sometimes unspeakable pain. Job considers himself to be one of them. In passionate self-defence he pleads his innocence (cf. 9.15–23). He cannot accept the 'justice' of his lot in which he is condemned in order to justify God.

---

9 Gutierrez, *On Job*, p. 29.

To Job, the God of the official theology is nothing other than a sadistic tyrant.[10] He can only protest against this type of God. In many images Job characterizes this tyrannical God. God 'crushes' Job 'with a tempest' and 'multiplies' his 'wounds' (9.17), 'as a lion' he hunts him (10.16) and brings 'fresh troops' against him to overpower him (10.17). Like Pharaoh in Egypt, God uses 'taskmasters' to exact the toil from his 'slaves' (3.18f.). God 'oppresses' (10.3), 'destroys' (10.8), 'breaks in two' (16.12) and 'slashes open' (16.13), he 'shuts in, deceives, and makes fools of' (12.14ff.), and lets 'leaders wander in a pathless waste' (12.24). With this God there is no difference between the innocent and the guilty, his choice is only 'violence' and not 'justice' (19.6f.):

> It is all one; therefore I say,
> he destroys both the blameless and the wicked.
> When disaster brings sudden death,
> he mocks at the calamity of the innocent. (Job 9.22f.)

Job is not a patient submissive sufferer, but a rebellious believer who protests against a theology which justifies suffering. You cannot justify God by condemning the innocent. But Job does not only protest against the theology of his friends the 'miserable comforters' (13.4; 16.1–6; 19.1–5); he also approaches God directly and challenges him to tell him why he has decided to punish him:

> If I sin, what do I do to you,
> you watcher of humanity?
> Why have you made me your target?
> Why have I become a burden to you? (Job 7.20)

As in a court of law, Job accuses God and demands that he should speak himself and explain why he is treating Job in this way (cf. 9.27–31; 10.2–22; 31.35–37). Job wants to argue his case and is certain that he will be vindicated (13.3, 18ff.).

In talking *to* God and no longer *about* him, Job realizes more

---

10 Sölle, *Leiden*, p. 141.

and more that only a living encounter with God himself will enable him to endure his incomprehensible and meaningless suffering.[11] The God of Job's friends is silent and inscrutable, but Job yearns to meet the God who speaks and who answers him:

> Oh, that I knew where I might find him,
> that I might come even to his dwelling!
> I would lay my case before him,
> and fill my mouth with arguments.
> I would learn what he would answer me,
> and understand what he would say to me. (Job 23.3–9)

It is to God himself, therefore, to whom he addresses his laments and complaints. As in many Old Testament psalms, Job wants God to see his pain and to hear his complaints. He reminds God that God himself created him, gave him skin and flesh, and granted him life in his steadfast love. He should not now forget that life had been the purpose of his creation (10.9–13).

Complaining and lamenting, for Job, is a form of expressing his hope and faith in God in spite of his own experience to the contrary. In the midst of his own unbearable pain he appeals to God himself to act as a mediator against the tyrannical God whom he experiences:

> O earth, do not cover my blood;
> let my outcry find no resting-place.
> Even now, in fact, my witness is in heaven,
> and he that vouches for me is on high.
> My friends scorn me;
> my eye pours out tears to God,
> that he would maintain the right of a mortal with God,
> as one does for a neighbour. (Job 16.18–21)

As a good neighbour would intervene if his friend is unjustly treated, so God should intervene and save Job from God's own

---

11 Gutierrez, *On Job*, p. 54.

unjust persecution. Job trusts that God as his true friend and saviour will lead him out of his imprisonment to freedom.

> For I know that my Redeemer lives,
> and that at the last he will stand upon the earth;
> and after my skin has been thus destroyed,
> then in my flesh I shall see God,
> whom I shall see on my side,
> and my eyes shall behold, and not another. (Job 19.25–27)

Although Job still accepts the basic premise of the doctrine of retribution that God judges human beings according to their deeds, he has found a different approach to the mystery of his suffering. 'My Redeemer lives.' God's compassion and willingness to save is greater than his 'justice'. This is true, in spite of all the clever and logically irrefutable arguments of his friends.

God finally answers Job. Job's desire to meet God and to hear him speak is fulfilled, though not in the way he had expected. The mystery of suffering, the question why he had to endure all the pain, the issue of the justice or injustice of all his misfortunes is not solved. God points to the mysteriousness of his creation which transcends all human understanding (Job 38–41). There are no 'solutions' to the problem of suffering, but through this personal encounter with God Job is changed:

> I had heard of you by the hearing of the ear,
> but now my eye sees you. (Job 42.5)

Job finds the real comfort, which his friends the 'miserable comforters' could not give him, in this 'seeing' of God.

In the conclusion God reprimands Job's friends. 'You have not spoken of me what is right, as my servant Job' (Job 42.7). The learned discourse of Job's friends was not 'right'. Those who felt the need to talk about God, and defend him and his justice, are now the accused and need the intercession of the rebellious Job (42.8). Job in his violent accusations, his passionate protest and complaints, spoke to God, and that was 'right'. In this, Job's hope for a vindicator, a redeemer, was fulfilled.

Conclusion

What are the implications of the Job paradigm for the counselling of AIDS patients?

Let me summarize the three main issues of this paper.

One of the basic conditions for patients to cope with their suffering and not to stay isolated and imprisoned in their own misery, is to find an adequate language. Counsellors must assist their patients by offering biblical paradigms which will enable them to develop that language. But religious language is ambivalent, it can be liberatory or repressive. The story of Job is a good example of the ambivalent nature of religious language. For AIDS patients the close link between deed and consequence is particularly acute. The questions, 'Why does this happen to me? Have I earned this punishment?' will be raised again and again. In this situation the counsellor can easily be pushed into the role of Job's friends, wishing to defend God and his justice against the complaints of the suffering person. The counsellor will then be tempted to talk about God and his justice in abstract terms and lose sight of the concrete situation of misery and despair of the patient. Job passionately objects to the doctrine that suffering is punishment for individual sins. The whole book of Job demonstrates that the justice of God cannot be measured according to a human yardstick and that God does not need human apology. In spite of the detailed theological exposition of God's justice given by his friends, Job does not find an answer which enables him to cope with his suffering. The counsellor should therefore recognize that the connection between human deeds and their consequences and the role which God plays in this connection are incomprehensible and that ultimately no intellectual or theological interpretation can unravel and give meaning to the problem of suffering.

The language of suffering people in the Bible, not only in the book of Job but also in the Psalms, is not abstract theological discourse but direct speech, the language of complaint which honestly gives expression to the pain as it is, and also the language of protest and even accusation. Job does not hesitate to accuse the mysterious hidden God who is ultimately responsible for his suffering. But he also dares to appeal to God the

Redeemer against this cruel God to help and to save him. Accusation and reproach is an integral part of this dialogue between Job and his God, as it is an essential element in many psalms of lament. The counsellor of AIDS patients should therefore allow this to happen and refrain from censuring it as impious talk, as Job's friends did. Using the language of protest and lament may very well be the first step for the patient to cope with his or her situation.

The real comfort in suffering can only come through the encounter with God himself. The problem for the patient is how to believe in God's presence in a situation which seems to suggest God's absence and wrath. This is the crucial test for the counsellor. Can he or she communicate with the patient in such a way that the patient can transcend feelings of isolation and rejection, and experience God's presence and acceptance? God's presence cannot be deduced from a demonstration of his omnipotence, i.e. the fact that the patient is healed from his or her sickness. Job is healed when he is able to confess: 'I had heard of you by the hearing of the ear, but now my eyes see you' (Job 42.5). The concluding report on his restoration to health and his former state of prosperity is taken from the popular narrative, but is not really necessary for the dialogues. Within the context of Old Testament faith the external sign of the reality of the inner healing and change of the person is still necessary. In the New Testament, God's power and omnipotence are believed in the suffering and death of the crucified Jesus of Nazareth. Now the experience of God's grace is sufficient, 'for power is made perfect in weakness' (2 Corinthians 12.9), even in a situation where there is no hope of physical healing.

12. Bioethics, AIDS, Theology and Social Change

LISA SOWLE CAHILL

Theological luminaries such as Paul Ramsey, Richard McCormick and James Gustafson were visible figures in the shaping of the new bioethics. As a result of their efforts, in co-operation with philosophers, medical doctors and researchers, the practice of biomedicine in the United States shifted directions. It moved decisively toward respect for patient autonomy and informed consent, and toward the formation of public policies, laws and judicial precedents to govern aspects of practice such as research on human subjects and decisions about life-sustaining treatment.

In the last ten or fifteen years, however, the complaint has often been registered that theology has lost influence in 'public' bioethics. The waning authority of religious voices has been attributed primarily to a growing reluctance of theologians to speak in a clearly religious voice, as they cede power to a 'thin' and 'secular' discourse that limits its moral claims to minimal requirements of procedural justice. Meanwhile, healthcare dollars are increasingly directed away from under-served populations; scientists and investors proceed with threats to 'human dignity', like stem cell research and human cloning, anticipating profit-making benefits for the wealthy. Theologians and religious communities are portrayed as guilty bystanders on the cultural road to perdition, down which biotech corporations and consumers are travelling at breakneck speed. The challenge to theology, on this analysis, is to recover its religiously distinctive prophetic voice, enter into policy debates more energetically, and persuade those with some control over policy outcomes to adopt a more prudent course and cautious pace.

After considering this critique, this chapter will argue that the real conflict is not between 'thin' and 'thick' moral languages and views of the good, but between competing 'thick' world-views and visions of ultimacy, complete with concepts of sin and salvation, good and evil, saints and sinners, liturgies and moral practices. It will examine both the appeal and the short-comings of the worldview governing biotech innovation today, with special reference to the area of genetics, then explore some theological alternatives. The thesis of the chapter will be that 'theological bioethics' is not so nerveless and enervated an enterprise as some of its critics make out, nor is it so marginal to current biomedical practice and policy. However, the impact and potential of theological bioethics can only be seen and appreciated if one's vision is broadened beyond the realms of academia and high-level government regulation. Although these are the spheres in which early bioethics made its name, they today do little to deter the profit-driven race for biotech innovation. The reality of theological bioethics certainly includes scholarship and policy, but its roots and much of its potential influence lie in broader and deeper networks that can exert pressure on research science, healthcare policy and biotech investment.

For this reason, theological bioethics can draw on work already done on local and global social movements favouring peace making and reconciliation, women's rights and economic participation. Activism and analysis surrounding AIDS drugs and genetically modified foods provide particularly close paral-lels to the availability of genetic developments in health care. Indeed, literature describing forms of 'participatory democracy' and of transnational global advocacy and global governance can be tied to categories more traditionally employed by theologians and religious communities ('solidarity', 'contribu-tive justice', 'subsidiarity', 'casuistry' and 'middle axioms', for example). It can support the hopeful claims of theologians and religious activists that change toward more just societies is actually possible.

Theological bioethics as it addresses genetics research is a good lens through which to examine this possibility. The new genomics (50 years after the discovery of DNA) is just emerging, is appearing under the morally attractive aegis of health benefits for 'humanity', but is also growing to maturity in an era in which globalization exacerbates inequities in access to resources. The fact that both economic globalization and genomics are rapidly changing domains, however, offers a window of opportunity for theologians and religious activists to have an impact on the ethical global governance of biotechnology and on the future allocation of healthcare resources.

At the present time, the health benefits of genetics research are more prospective than real. The directions in which they are developing are largely determined by perceived 'need', i.e. market demand. People who have access to basic nutrition, hygiene and health care, and who do not run a high risk of early death from communicable diseases such as malaria and tuberculosis, are interested in genetic diagnosis and treatment for cancer, cardiovascular disease, dementia and diseases with a clear link to specific genes (such as Huntington's disease and cystic fibrosis). The World Health Organization (WHO) estimates that pneumonia, diarrhoea, tuberculosis and malaria, which account for over 20% of the world's disease burden, receive less than 1% of the total public and private health research funds. Of the 1,233 new drugs marketed between 1975 and 1999, only 13 were approved specifically for tropical diseases, and six of these were developed under special grants from the WHO and United Nations Development Program.[1]

In the case of diseases which strike both rich and poor, and for which genetic diagnosis or treatments are available, or in the process of development – such as thalassemia and diabetes – access to genetic interventions is dependent upon ability to pay. Thalassemia is under control in the US and Europe, but in most other countries of the world, thousands of children a year die of this condition. Diabetes is on the rise globally, and genomic research is moving toward therapy; but there is no more reason to expect that the benefits will be any more available to

---

1 World Health Organization Advisory Committee on Health Research, 2002, Minutes, p. 17.

impoverished families than are tests for thalassemia or AIDS drugs. Meanwhile, evidence mounts that knowledge of the genomics of pathogens could lead to much more effective prevention and treatment of communicable diseases like malaria, tuberculosis, dengue fever, meningitis B, hepatitis B, and even African AIDS.[2] Yet funding for the necessary research is not plentiful, and access to benefits is very constrained for the majority of the world's population. This will be even more true of 'luxury' or 'discretionary' genetic services, such as enhancement of 'normal' traits.

Right now, clean water, food, basic health care perinatal care, and the AIDS pandemic are of mightier concern in most cultures than genomics. Questions of justice in the development of genetic medicine thus arise in at least the following areas: more equitable health resource allocation in general, nationally and globally; shaping the future applications of genetic medicine so that rich and poor are served; and the possible redistribution or 'sharing' of profits from genetic biotechnologies so that 'advances' aimed at a first world market will contribute to a rise in health in the developing world. It will here be argued that theological and religious traditions prioritize distributive justice as the moral consequence of religious identity; that religious traditions have in the past and can presently and in the future mobilize democratic social participation and change; and that theology and religion have significant roles to play in 'public' debates and policies on health care in general and genetics in particular.

Three or four decades ago, theologians like Paul Ramsey, James Gustafson, Richard McCormick,[3] and Karen Lebacqz served on national policy-changing bodies such as the National Commission on the Protection of Human Subjects of Biomedical and Behavioral Research (1974) and the President's Commission for the Study of Ethical Problems in Medicine and

---

2 World Health Organization Advisory Committee on Health Research, 2002, Minutes, pp. 12–16.

3 See further Lisa Sowle Cahill, 2001, 'Religion and Theology' in Jeremy Sugarman and Daniel P. Sulmasy OFM (eds), *Methods in Medical Ethics*, Washington, DC: Georgetown University Press.

Biomedical and Behavioral Research (1979). Theologians were among the highly visible figures who founded and worked in bioethics institutes such as the Institute of Religion at the Texas Medical Center in Houston (1954); the Institute of Society, Ethics and the Life Sciences, later to become the Hastings Center (1961); and the Kennedy Institute of Ethics at Georgetown University (1971). Theologians of the time not only were addressing problems in applied ethics with more focus and frequency than philosophers; they also came from long-standing communities of reflection on basic human enigmas like the meanings of life, death and suffering.

These early theological participants in bioethics debates were not hesitant to use religious imagery, arguments and principles. For example, Gustafson defined the contributions of theology to medical ethics by lifting out three themes: God intends the well-being of the creation; God preserves and orders the creation, as well as creates new possibilities; and humans are finite and sinful agents who have great power to determine whether the well-being of the creation is sustained or not.[4] Yet Gustafson saw theologians as adopting different modes of discourse at different times, for different purposes. These could include narrative, prophetic and ethical forms that were explicitly rooted in theological premises; they also included types of ethical and policy discourse that were not. Policy discourse in particular requires persons with institutional roles to formulate options and recommendations within the available limits and possibilities, both in terms of the practical adjustments that are feasible and the argumentation that will be persuasive.[5]

Paul Ramsey, an ardent champion of a biblical, covenantal ethic, used creation imagery from the Prologue to John's Gospel to argue against reproductive technologies.[6] However, in addressing the British government with testimony against *in*

---

4 James F. Gustafson, 1975, *The Contributions of Theology to Medical Ethics*, Milwaukee: Marquette University Theology Department, pp. 19–22.

5 James F. Gustafson, 1996, *Intersections: Science, Theology and Ethics*, Cleveland: The Pilgrim Press, pp. 35–55.

6 Paul Ramsey, 1970, *Fabricated Man: The Ethics of Genetic Control*, New Haven and London: Yale University Press, p. 88.

vitro fertilization, his language was not overtly theological. Instead, he appealed to a humane sense of the dignity and goods of parenthood, and predicted 'further assaults upon the natural foundations of the integrity of the marriage relation, and new ways toward the manufacture of children'.[7] Similarly, the Catholic theologian Richard McCormick was attentive to the 'Christian conviction that the sexual love that generates ought to become in principle the parental love that nurtures'.[8] However, he argued against donor insemination on the basis of what he regarded as a human appreciation of marriage and parenthood: it 'separates procreation from marriage, or the procreative sphere from the sphere of marital love, in a way that is either violative of the marriage covenant or likely to be destructive of it and the family'.[9]

By the end of the 1970s, bioethics enjoyed great cultural credibility, according to Daniel Callahan, founder, with Willard Gaylin, of the Hastings Center.[10] This came about because most bioethicists adopted an 'interesting and helpful' approach to biomedical dilemmas, rather than railing against the establishment, and also because 'they were quite willing to talk in a fully secular way'. In fact, bioethics became popular because it was able 'to push religion aside'.[11] This, according to critics, was precisely what led theologians in bioethics eventually to lose their influence. Theologians succumbed to the pressure to frame the issues and to speak 'in a common secular mode'.[12] Religion became intimidated from 'speaking in its own voice', or came to be viewed as able to speak with integrity only within 'the confines of particular religious communities'.[13]

---

7 Paul Ramsey, 1984, 'The Issues Facing Mankind' in J. Lejeune, P. Ramsey and G. Wright (eds), *The Question of In Vitro Fertilization: Studies in Medicine, Law and Ethics*, London: The SPUC Educational Trust, p. 26.

8 Richard A. McCormick SJ, 1981, *How Brave a New World*, New York: Doubleday, p. 321.

9 McCormick, *How Brave a New World*, p. 317.

10 Daniel Callahan, 1993, 'Why America Accepted Bioethics', *The Hastings Center Report* 23:6, p. S8.

11 Callahan, 'Why America Accepted Bioethics', p. S8.

12 Daniel Callahan, 1990, 'Religion and the Secularization of Bioethics', *The Hastings Center Report* 20, p. S3.

13 Callahan, 'Religion and the Secularization of Bioethics', p. S4.

Among others, John H. Evans, who focuses especially on genetic science, laments the ascendancy of an approach to bioethics centred on the four 'secular' principles of autonomy, beneficence, non-maleficence and justice.[14] Evans employs a distinction between 'thick' and 'thin' theories of the good that ultimately goes back to John Rawls.[15] Rawls distinguished between a 'thin' and a 'fuller' theory of the good in order to get people to come to the table of public decision-making agreed that certain primary goods should be secured for all in a just society. He maintained that social inequalities are just only in so far as they work to secure these primary goods for society's least favoured members.[16] Evans' complaint is that the consequent 'thinning' of public debate has 'eviscerated' the discourse needed to make important decisions about whether human genetic engineering is compatible with worthy societal ends, since discussion of those ends is ruled out of bounds in the first place.

In his view, the policy discourse on genetic engineering in the United States is both exemplified and shaped by *Splicing Life* (1983), a report of a presidential advisory commission on genetic engineering. The commission entertained the concerns of theologians and religious leaders about the aims of genetic engineering and its ultimate effects on human life and on societies. Yet the final report termed the theological concerns 'vague', and focused on more concrete problems (e.g. creating animal–human hybrids) that the theological objections could not definitively resolve. Thus the concerns that the creation of new life-forms oversteps the boundaries of prudence and humility, or that the poor are being left behind in the development of genetic technologies, are left out of account in the final reckoning of the ethics and legality of genetic engineering.[17] Evans

---

14 John H. Evans, 2002, *Playing God? Human Genetic Engineering and the Rationalization of Public Bioethical Debate*, Chicago and London: University of Chicago Press, p. 88.

15 John Rawls, 1971, *A Theory of Justice*, Cambridge MA: Harvard University Press, pp. 395–9; see also John Rawls, 1993, *Political Liberalism*, New York: Columbia University Press, pp. 178–95.

16 Rawls, *A Theory of Justice*, p. 396.

17 Evans, *Playing God?*, pp. 127–31.

maintains that more recent debates over cloning have served to consolidate the formal rationality of 'bioethics', and to further eliminate 'thick' traditions and perspectives on the larger ends of biomedicine from public debate. Instead, autonomy has become an unexamined end in itself, and few if any limits have been imposed by law or regulation on the adventures of science.[18]

Evans' ideal, for which he believes the prospects to be bleak, is for citizens to listen to professional debates about genetic engineering, take their concerns back to their 'thick' communities of belief and value, and then bring the 'demands' of their group regarding ends 'to the public's elected officials'.[19] To reinvigorate public debate, he recommends that separate commissions be established to deal with societal ends, and with means to ends. Professionals might serve on the latter, but not the former. These commissions might solicit public participation through local consultations and surveys, possibly adapting the model used by the State of Oregon to determine the medical procedures that would be covered under Medicaid. Evans cites the burgeoning 'participatory democracy' literature to bolster his case.[20]

In my view, Evans is on the right track in suggesting that greater public participation in bioethical debates would more fully engage the members of religious traditions and other groups whose perspectives do not find a comfortable home in the discourse of 'professional' bioethics. At the same time, it is striking that he and other critics of the secularization of bioethics keep their gaze so firmly fixed on governmental bodies such as public commissions, regulatory agencies, and legislatures. Not only are the decisions and policies of such bodies the ultimate target of influence, they are also expected to play a major role in the reinvigoration of the discourses that they are claimed to have suppressed. No wonder Evans' expectation of change is modest. And Evans is not alone; in fact he

18 Evans, *Playing God?*, pp. 158–65.
19 Evans, *Playing God?*, p. 197.
20 See Amy Gutman and Dennis Thompson, 1996, *Democracy and Disagreement*, Cambridge, MA: Harvard University Press.

represents the general assumptions of most of the literature on theology, bioethics and policy.

To a remarkable degree, the critics of 'the Enlightenment Project' of secular discourse have bought into the terms of that project when they agree that influential public discourse not only is secular but is controlled by intellectual and scientific elites who are privileged arbiters of the direction government will take. Michel Foucault used the term 'the repressive hypothesis' to refer to the way modern 'discourse' about sex co-opts everyone who discusses sex into the belief that their sexuality is under illegitimate constraints that must be thrown off. As a consequence, everyone behaves as if such constraints really existed, and, perversely obedient to the modern discourse that re-creates sex as 'sexuality', obsesses about sex as something that must at all costs be 'rediscovered', 'owned' and 'liberated'. In this way, the discourse of repression stimulates and proliferates the very reality supposedly constrained, even while convincing those engaged in it that its existence is precarious. Moreover, the reality produced (sex) follows norms of the controlling discourse (a scientific and therapeutic discourse), delegitimating countervailing experiences, values and norms.[21]

One might conclude the same about the supposed 'marginalization' of theology in bioethics, taking note of the number of papers and articles that have dealt with the phenomenon in the past 15 or more years. The parallel with Foucault's analysis of sexual 'repression' is especially striking, in light of the never-ending advocacy of many churches, religious groups and theologians for 'pro-life' causes. The prevailing discourse has managed virtually to equate 'religious bioethics' with such advocacy, constructing it as a public danger, even while insisting on its marginality. An important corollary is that the 'official' discourse also establishes the bioethics issues that will be central to public policy. For public debate in law, policy, medicine and research, the focal issue is undoubtedly the protection of autonomy by procedural guarantees of informed consent. Meanwhile, religion is framed as entirely preoccupied

---

21 Michel Foucault, 1978, *The History of Sexuality*, Vol. 1, New York: Random House, pp. 3–49.

with 'status of life' issues, especially the fate of embryos and the processes of reproduction, and as in the grip of a vaguely articulated and ultimately baseless fear that interference with 'natural' reproduction will denigrate 'human dignity'. Leaving aside the possible merit of such concerns, an equally or more important concern of religion and theology – the economics of biotech development and genomics and their effects on social solidarity and distributive justice – is quite effectively kept off the policy table by the dominant discourse, and its construction of 'mainstream' and 'marginal' voices. Religious thinkers, policy-makers and the public have, for the most part, conceded that religion and theology have very little ultimate effect on what really goes on in biomedicine and research, and that even laws and policy that appear to set limits will eventually give way in the face of scientific 'advances' and corporate demands.

The disenfranchisement of theological bioethics is sealed by theologians' concession of their own irrelevance; theologians' complaint that secular thinking has squeezed them out of the public realm in fact abets the very worldview that displaces theology. The narrative of the exclusion of 'religion' helps conceal the fact that 'secular' bioethics is in fact deeply and extensively tradition based and 'thick' with the imagery and language of transcendent meaning. Like other forms of transcendent experience and worship, science and genetics are grounded in communal practices, imaginatively nourished by mythologies and saints, justified by ideologies of purpose, warned against outer demons and inner sinfulness, and urged to keep the faith with promises of salvation.

While public theological bioethics has typically focused its energies on government regulation and legislation as means to control genetic developments, traditions of Christian social activism and new studies of participatory democracy and participatory, democratic global governance may in combination suggest new directions for theological analysis of bioethics and social change. A few theologians note, specifically in regard to the practice and social institutionalization of genomics, that the many mediating institutions of public life provide opportunities for theological impact beyond the more visible debate on legislation, policies and funding. Everyone in civil society lives in many overlapping associations where values are formed that affect the common life. Andrew Lustig draws on communitarian construals of public engagement, in which 'various forms of suasion and moral authority' are at work in the conversation, in which 'extra-legal sanctions' for decisions and practices could be developed. Theological bioethicists themselves work in a variety of more and less formal professional capacities, including ethics committees, institutional review boards, advisory commissions and professional advisers.[22]

It is possible to extend and deepen the connection of theological bioethics to social activism by linking religion and theology to coalitions working for distributive justice on multiple levels, from community organizing to national legislation to transnational advocacy networks. Resources include studies of participatory democracy in the US, as well as participatory global governance; many participatory social movements are sponsored in whole or part by faith traditions or ecumenical organizations. Catholicism stands out as having a more long-standing institutional presence in health care, as well as a substantial teaching tradition on social justice issues, including health resource allocation, and a track record of activism to empower disenfranchised groups.[23] These achievements find parallels in Protestant Christianity and other religions, including the Social Gospel, temperance, women's suffrage and civil rights movements, and more contemporary projects that include health care and genetics.[24]

The concepts of casuistry and virtue (see Chapter 14) clarify why theology can rarely provide master theories for bioethics policy or definitive resolutions of dilemmas and value conflicts. Rather, theology and religion nurture a social and intellectual

---

22 Andrew B. Lustig, 2001, 'Human Cloning and Liberal Neutrality: Why We Need to Broaden the Public Dialogue' in M. J. Hanson (ed.), *Claiming Power Over Life: Religion and Biotechnology Policy*, Washington, DC: Georgetown University Press, p. 47.

23 Clarke E. Cochrane and David Carroll Cochrane, 2003, *Catholics, Politics and Public Policy: Beyond Left and Right*, Maryknoll, NY: Orbis, chapter 3.

24 See Audrey R. Chapman, 1999, *Unprecedented Choices: Religious Ethics at the Frontiers of Genetic Science*, Minneapolis: Fortress Press.

milieu in which the social priorities of religious communities can be recognized sympathetically. Social practices and policy outcomes are more likely to reflect respect for all human lives and a 'preferential option for the poor' if religious thinkers represent these values while engaging with others in the practical negotiation of solutions to shared problems.

A striking example from the healthcare realm is a series of events that in about a two-year period loosened the grip of major pharmaceutical companies on patented AIDS drugs, making them available cheaply or for free in countries with high rates both of poverty and of AIDS deaths, beginning with South Africa. In this particular example, religious voices, local activism, NGOs, the UN, market competition from generic drug manufacturers, and market pressure from consumers and stockholders, all played some part, resulting in a modification of World Trade Organization policy on intellectual property, over which the power of big business had seemed unassailable at the start.[25] Again, the lesson for theological bioethics is that social change is possible even when the entrenched systems of control over goods are infected with structural sin. Forceful intervention can be accomplished co-operatively, along a spectrum of pressure points, even in the absence of commitment from top-level arbiters of law and policy.

---

25 See further: David Barnard, 'In the High Court of South Africa, Case No. 4138/98: The Global Politics of Access to Lower-Cost AIDS Drugs in Poor Countries', *Kennedy Institute of Ethics Journal* 12, pp. 159–74; Samantha Power, 'The AIDS Rebel', *The New Yorker*, 19 May 2003, pp. 54–67; and Lisa Sowle Cahill, 2003, 'Biotech Justice: Catching Up with the Real World Order', *Hastings Center Report* 33:4, pp. 39–42.

13. AIDS Prevention and the Lesser Good

LEONARD M. MARTIN

In many circles, especially church circles, the expression 'education is the best prevention' operates as a slogan, almost as a mantra. There is a feeling that if we can get the right information across to young people especially, and if we can get them to adopt what we perceive as being correct attitudes and values, then the struggle to prevent AIDS is well on the right path. It is important to note, however, that education is not a magic formula that automatically brings results. Information, adequately divulged, and training people young and old to develop certain attitudes and skills in inter-personal relationships, can undoubtedly bring about reasonably satisfactory results as far as AIDS prevention is concerned, but they are not an infallible remedy. In view of that, while one can certainly say that investment in information and education is a good thing, it would be naïve to rely *exclusively* on publicity campaigns and occasional educational programmes in schools as a means of preventing the spread of AIDS.

Raising awareness as to the nature of the disease and as to how it is transmitted can certainly save lives, and as such should be promoted and supported. Educating young people to value monogamy, fidelity and the sanctity of marriage is certainly an important step towards containing the AIDS epidemic. Morally speaking, it would seem to me a safe position to affirm that there exists a general obligation to inform people about AIDS and educate them in humanizing values so that they can take measures to protect themselves and their loved ones from contamination. By the same token, we can affirm that people have the obligation to inform and to form themselves. The obligation is not only to teach, but also to learn. But it is not enough to know. Prevention is also about choosing behaviour patterns and implementing them.

Teaching and learning about AIDS are undoubtedly important and beneficial, but information on its own does not guarantee that people will change how they think or how they feel. The strength of this approach is that it appeals to the rational side of people, to their intelligence and to their prudence. The weakness of this approach is that it fails to take into account the fact that people do not always do what they know is best, nor even what they know is right. A further weakness is that it underestimates a very potent mix, which is the combination of desire and fascination with what is prohibited and with what is dangerous. People of all ages are no strangers to the pulls of *eros* and *thanatos*, but for young people especially the attractions are particularly potent, and the urge to court the limits of life, love and death is very much part of the process of growing up. A certain sense of invulnerability, that 'it cannot happen to me', seems to be part of the adolescent mind-set and this guarantees limited efficacy to warnings about the dangers of certain types of behaviour. If anything, the warnings can have a reverse impact, increasing the fascination with the forbidden and the dangerous.

Education has, undoubtedly, an important role in the area of AIDS prevention and there is an obligation to both teach and learn about the subject, but its limitations force us to take a closer look at what we might call the ethics of prophylactics: medical, social and sexual.

Within the area of *medical prophylactics*, it makes a great deal of sense for health professionals to take precautions against coming into contact with contaminated fluids. It makes sense both technically and ethically for a dentist to use protective gloves and glasses in procedures where there may be contact with blood or saliva. There is a general obligation for him or her to take normal care not to be exposed to unnecessary risks. By the same token, there is not just a technical requirement but also an ethical imperative to use sterilized instruments because there also exists an obligation to protect the client and not expose him or her to unnecessary danger of contamination.

As an example of *social prophylactics*, we can speak of programmes designed to help drug addicts avoid contamination. Among these initiatives, one of the most polemical is that of providing drug users with sterilized needles with a view to preventing needle swapping. There is here clearly a technical dimension, where one can raise the question as to the efficacy of the procedure – does this method in fact work as a way of reducing contamination through needle sharing? – but there is also here an ethical dimension. Does the good achieved truly outweigh the possible harms that may follow? Can one safely say that this practice does not increase the use of injected illegal drugs through making needles and syringes more readily available, and so increasing the harm done?

These are all significant ethical questions. The thorniest ethical questions, especially from a church point of view, arise, however, in relation to dilemmas raised by *sexual prophylactics*. In this area, one of the first difficulties that ethical discourse has to face is that of *credibility*. There is a certain form of ethical discourse that takes a position, which is from the very start non-negotiable, to the effect that all genital–sexual activity outside of marriage is wrong. People who have been brought up in a Catholic ethos, where the sanctity of marriage has been held in high esteem and where not only consecrated chastity but also chastity before marriage and during courtship have also been held in high regard, have a reasonably good chance of understanding this discourse, even if they do not always live according to its dictates. Very many people, however, whether living in postmodern Europe or the United States or in a whole gamut of Latin American cultures, whether modern or pre- or postmodern, for a variety of reasons, simply find this type of language difficult to understand and its demands unrealistic. Since the sublime ideal of perfect sexual continence before marriage seems to them not only unintelligible but impracticable, they draw the conclusion that religious people in general and Catholic moral theology in particular has nothing more to say to them.

We are witnessing, in this reaction, one of the great evils of moral rigorism – the fact that it tends to provoke generalized laxism: since only the highest of ideals are acceptable and intermediary efforts count for nothing, then there is nothing more to be said or done and there is no point in lesser efforts which will be deemed to be of no value. Taken into the field of sexual ethics, this mentality would follow the line that since total sexual abstinence before marriage is not possible, and since it and only it is deemed acceptable, then there is no point in any type of restraint. Masturbation becomes an acceptable adolescent pastime and recreational sex a legitimate occupation between consenting adults, provided, of course, that they practise 'safe sex'. Even for those who have a residual religious conscience, the attitude would tend to be that of the old English saying, dating from the time when sheep stealing was a capital offence: 'You may as well be hanged for a sheep as a lamb', or to put it in more apocalyptic terms: if you are going to hell, it may as well be for a decent mortal sin!

If ethics is to overcome this credibility gap and not abandon people to a moral laxism that undermines all attempts to promote an approach to human sexuality based on a natural law that gives value to the person and respect and concern for the dignity of the other, it must present challenges that strike people as achievable and find new ways to express these challenges that are intelligible to the people addressed.

It is fundamental to recognize that we have here a plurality of subjects whose discourse is situated within a plurality of cultural paradigms, each with its own worldview and sets of behaviour models. If people within a particular cultural paradigm, for example a Catholic one, wish to have an impact on people who have another worldview and who subscribe to specific models of behaviour which differ from those found in the various Catholic paradigms, then they must awake to the necessity of using means of communication and persuasion that are appropriate to the task.

By and large, however, Catholic church authorities have shied away from the challenges of entering into the worldview of people with whom they disagree. They have relied instead on repeating insistently formulae and positions that are intelligible and coherent within their own frame of reference, but without making any real effort to understand, communicate and persuade, using the tried and tested missionary methods of inculturation, respectful listening, dialogue and the search for common ground on which to build that portion of the Kingdom of God which may be brought about while in a desert wandering, even when the promised land is a distant and as yet unattainable future dream. There has been some effort within Catholic circles to do this, bringing into the AIDS arena the discussion of the double effect and the lesser evil[1] and with the publication of an important study, involving theologians from around the world, *Catholic Ethicists on HIV/AIDS Prevention*.[2] We would suggest that there is still a long way to go.

Though there is a long way to go, there are, however, signs of hope. In many church documents of recent times there is an important balance between concern for expressing moral truth in a doctrinally rigorous way and pastoral concern for people. I myself have demonstrated this with regards to the question of homosexuality in a submission made, at committee stage, to a bill passing through the Brazilian parliament.[3] The difficulty is that church people, both clerical and lay, often fail badly when it comes to communicating this subtle, but important balance and so end up projecting an understanding of sexual morality, especially, that is one-sided and which fails to do justice to the complexity of the Catholic tradition.

Where this distortion comes out clearly is in the almost morbid preoccupation that some people have with sin, while relegating to a secondary place, or forgetting altogether the love of a God who first loved us, who calls us to share his life, who respects our liberty because he wants our love with all its limitations and who proved his love for us, and his patience, sending his Son to show us the way we should walk should we want to use our liberty to reciprocate his love.

---

1 Brian V. Johnstone CSsR, 'AIDS Prevention and the Lesser Evil', *Studia Moralia* XXXIX:1, June 2001, pp. 197–216.

2 James F. Keenan SJ *et al.* (ed.), 2000, *Catholic Ethicists of HIV/AIDS Prevention*, London and New York: Continuum.

3 See Leonard M. Martin CSsR, 'A Homossexualidade numa Perspectiva Cristã: Subsídios para Avaliação do Projeto de Lei no 1.151, de 1995', *Espaços – Revista Semestral de Teologia*, 5:1, 1997, pp. 15–36.

The search for moral truth and for doctrinal rigour is poorly served when we lose sight of the pastoral concern for people which is an indispensable hermeneutical element in the proclamation of that truth. The splendour of truth is poorly served by using a filter which seeks out only what is evil, what is sin, what is failure and by not using a filter which permits one to identify the good that people do or are capable of doing within situations which fall far short of the sublime ideal proposed by the gospel but which reflect the little good that can be done in the here and now. People often find themselves in the desert rather than in the promised land through no fault of their own. Instead of reinforcing their exclusion, the challenge is how to build on what is to hand and to explore the good that is possible while waiting patiently for the day of perfection to dawn.

Even within the sin and evil filter there is a growing awareness that the doctrine of the lesser evil can point the way to a more positive search for the attainable practical ideal and for the lesser good that can effectively be done.

Brian Johnstone has been particularly helpful in this regard in his recent article to which we have already referred in passing. In his quick review of the history of the appeal to the principle of the lesser evil, he finds precedents in Aristotle, Augustine, Aquinas and St Alphonsus. Aristotle followed Plato in thinking that soldiers would be better fighters if they did not marry, but then went on to observe that since they are prone to sexual indulgence, 'it is a lesser evil to have carnal intercourse with women than to fall into homosexual practices',[4] Augustine thought that prostitutes should be tolerated 'because they fulfil a similar function in society to that of the cesspool in the palace'.[5] Johnstone quotes him as saying, rather unflatteringly, of one of the oldest professions: 'Remove the cesspool and you will fill the palace with filth. Take away prostitutes from the world and you will fill it with sodomy.'[6]

One of the most striking texts within the lesser evil tradition is also from Augustine. Speaking of the case where a man is con-

---

4 Johnstone, 'AIDS Prevention', p. 212.
5 Johnstone, 'AIDS Prevention', p. 212.
6 Johnstone, 'AIDS Prevention', p. 212.

templating killing his wife so as to be free to marry another woman, he says: 'If a man is about to do what is not lawful, let him commit adultery and not homicide; and while his own wife lives, let him marry another and not shed human blood.'[7] Johnstone goes on to comment on this text saying: 'No doubt the author of the text would have agreed that the ideal course of action would be to convert the would-be wife murderer to a life of virtue and restored harmony with his partner. But the problem was that, in the circumstances, instant conversion was not possible and if some action were not taken immediately the wife would be dead and the husband would have made himself a murderer.'[8]

St Alphonsus comes to much the same conclusion, giving the status of 'more probable' to the view that counselling the lesser evil is solid practice. Applying this to the AIDS scene, Johnstone says: '. . . it could be argued that a counsellor may propose to a person infected with the HIV virus, who will not abstain from sexual activity, that he or she use a condom rather than risk transmitting the lethal virus, causing the death of the partner, and transforming himself into a culpable killer'.[9] Basically, he would seem to be saying that if someone is going to break the sixth commandment anyway, it is a good thing that he or she not break the fifth as well, intentionally exposing someone to infection with a deadly virus.

There is no question here of scandalously harming someone by the fact of encouraging him or her to do something evil. On the contrary, one is benefiting the perpetrator, helping him or her to avoid compacting the evil intended and hence lessening the guilt. The person may continue being guilty of a disordered sexual act, but at least he or she is not guilty of deliberate murder.

Within this context, respect for moral truth may well lead one to condemn the evil that is being done, to condemn the sin, but one must be very careful not to condemn the sinner in the

---

7 Johnstone, 'AIDS Prevention', p. 213.
8 Johnstone, 'AIDS Prevention', p. 213.
9 Johnstone, 'AIDS Prevention', p. 214.

process. A missionary morals[10] that is sensitive to the chains that bind people in their captivity and to shackles that slow them down as they tramp through the desert, will not deny the reality of chain and shackle, but will do every little thing it can to create what spaces of freedom are available and anticipate as much as present circumstances will permit the values of the promised land. It may be a pale reflection of the sublime ideal, but it is the practical ideal which is possible.

There is a further point which must be made. From an ecclesiastical perspective, the lesser evil may be a satisfactory solution, tying away loose ends and fitting neatly into the broad tradition, but, from the point of view of those who do not share that worldview, it can be patronizing and offensive. There are homosexual couples who do not consider the affection that they express for each other through genital contact as a lesser evil that protects them from promiscuity, though their relationship can be depicted in that light. They see no need to appeal to the double effect to justify their use of condoms, since the use to which they put them is prophylactic and certainly not contraceptive. They resent their physical love for each other being characterized as a lesser evil when they experience it as a good which cements a caring relationship and a self-giving which flows over into other spheres of life. What they may be open to discuss is that the form which their relationship takes is a lesser good, which falls short of the ideal of heterosexual love which is faithful, monogamous and fertile, but they would want to maintain recognition of the good that is present. While official church teaching or specific moral systems may find their behaviour morally lacking or even evil, pastoral and missionary concern requires one to remember that one of the divine longings is for everyone to be saved and to come to a knowledge of the truth. One of the divine longings is for everyone to be a saint

---

10 See Leonard M. Martin CSsR, 'Moral Missionária para o Novo Milênio', *Vida Pastoral* May–June 1997, pp. 23–9; also in *O Mundo da Saúde*, ano 22, 22:3, May–June 1998; also under the title 'Moral Missionária e Pastoral para um Novo Milênio' in Giuseppe Cinà *et al.* (org.), *Dicionário Interdisciplinar da Pastoral da Saúde* [Centro Universitário São Camilo/Paulus, São Paulo 199], pp. 813–20.

and to share in the life of God. Consequently, pastoral care cannot be separated from the proclamation of the truth, nor from respect for the integrity of people's consciences and for what they perceive to be good. For this very reason, there is a need to look beyond the lesser evil and look to the lesser good if one wants to appeal to the better instincts of people involved in behaviour which, for some, is intrinsically disordered, but for them is the lifestyle that has either been imposed on them by fate or has been freely chosen by them as the good they are currently capable of.

From this it is clear that it is not enough to counsel people to do the lesser evil. The challenge is to get them to do the good they are capable of, even if it falls far short of the sublime ideal of sexual continence outside of marriage and of loving, faithful and fruitful union within marriage.

The pursuit of the lesser good may not make for great saints, but it does make for little saints, those who follow Christ, limping along with the legs they have, climbing over the rough terrain where life has placed them, and, when they cannot quite make it, finding themselves carried in the arms of a loving father.

14. AIDS and a Casuistry of Accommodation

JAMES F. KEENAN

Because they have a set of moral teachings that claim to be absolutely exceptionless, Catholics love coming up with the exceptions. Thirty years ago, for instance, several moral theologians did not believe that the encyclical *Humanae Vitae* was right in its claim that every instance of artificial birth control was wrong. Not having to prove that every instance was right, many were only interested in challenging the claim that birth control was *always* wrong. They highlighted, therefore, the case of a mother of eight, whose heart condition threatened her survival and who would not live through another pregnancy. Her failure to use birth control was itself life threatening. Added to the case was the circumstance that abstinence was not an alternative; her careless husband scorned it. In the event of her likely death, her eight children plus the newborn would be left motherless; and given the carelessness of the father, the children would not be in good hands. The case was compelling, and it made its point: not every instance of artificial birth control was necessarily wrong.

Of course, Jesus too loved cases. By using parables, Jesus presented new insights. He persuaded us by the cases he made. He answered the famous question 'Who is my neighbour?' (Luke 10.29–37) with the case of the Good Samaritan. When faced with the charge that he ate with sinners, he gave the case of the prodigal son (Luke 15.2, 11–32). Jesus used cases not only to teach us but to persuade us. Cases are, after all, particu-

lar tools or instruments in the repertory of rhetorical arguments.[1]

Whether we talk of Jesus, Americans or Catholics, their
respective proclivities to casuistry have one thing in common:
they all trust in the function of the case method, where cases are
brief narratives or stories that we use to consider anew what we
may have missed when making other claims. Cases bring to our
attention a new claim that needs to be engaged.

The history of casuistry reveals that for the past four centuries Catholic moral logic has been faithful to its clear principles and at the same time has been consistently willing to
consider new cases, which it resolved without compromising
the existing material principles. It did this by a fairly broad
selection of methodological principles that allowed casuists to
recognize new claims that were not covered by the material
principles. Clearly, the method helped build up the Catholic
community as it negotiated over time new problems on the
horizon.[2]

The original function of the case method remains intact, then,
even in the fairly deductive type of logic based on principles
articulated three centuries ago. Today, we still entertain these
cases or narratives in order to consider what we may have
missed when making earlier claims. Through these methodological principles, casuists accommodated the new claims
while protecting the integrity of the principle. This balance
between preserving moral order and entertaining the chaos of
complicated pregnancies, complicated military strategies, complicated surgeries, complicated protocols for the dying, and
complicated reproductive technologies, has served the Catholic
community well over these four centuries.

---

1 I develop this in 'The Case for Physician Assisted Suicide', *America* 179,
1998, pp. 14–19; and in 'Cases, Rhetoric, and the American Debate about
Physician Assisted Suicide' in *Der medizinisch assistierte Tod. Zur Frage der
aktiven Sterbenhilfe*, ed. Adrian Holdregger, Herder, forthcoming.

2 See Thomas Kopfensteiner, 1995, 'Science, Metaphor and Moral
Casuistry' in James Keenan and Thomas Shannon (eds), *The Context of
Casuistry*, Washington, DC: Georgetown University Press, pp. 207–20;
and John T. Noonan Jr, 'The Development in Moral Doctrine', *Context*,
pp. 188–203.

Moreover, this balancing act was accomplished by a fairly sophisticated logic recognized and understood by the entire Catholic community. Church leaders did not claim we should avoid facing the claims of these complicated matters, lest we cause scandal. Theologians did not claim that we should not address the indirect abortions of an ectopic pregnancy because they could confuse the faithful on abortion; popes did not compromise the pain of the dying by claiming that they could not address it lest the faithful be confused over the Church's stance on euthanasia; and on no occasion did bishops reject tolerance of nuclear deterrence so as not to cause consternation about the community's apprehension of the principle of not directly killing the innocent. On the contrary, popes, bishops and theologians recognized that church members were well aware of the long-sustained logic that both appreciated ordered principles and took into account the complicating claims of new cases that often needed to be arbitrated by these methodological principles.

In contrast with this history, when we turn to investigating the relationship between casuistry and the topic of AIDS, we find something astonishing: a resistance by Catholic leadership to any theologian's casuistry about AIDS. To support this claim, I present three cases: the case of a healthcare worker in a Catholic healthcare facility facing a patient who has just tested HIV-positive and who has no intention of becoming sexually abstinent; the case of proposing needle exchange programmes; and the case of testing the HIV status of candidates applying to religious orders. In each of these cases, moral theologians have engaged in a casuistry that Catholic leadership actively resists; their resistance provides, however, a translucent glimpse of some underlying anxiety.

At the outset, we need to recognize that, for the most part, the casuistry being invoked in the face of AIDS is *not* generally speaking the more revolutionary sixteenth-century casuistry that sought to replace principles, but rather the casuistry that accommodates new cases while protecting existing principles. One exception is Kevin Kelly who asks the overarching question: why does Christian sexual ethics so often hamper rather than assist humanity as it faces the AIDS pandemic? His new book on moral theology and the challenge of AIDS attempts to offer new directions that sexual ethics needs to pursue in order to be at the service of all human beings.[3] Kelly aside, almost every other theologian's casuistic proposal is a more modest look at the present crisis. This is a very important insight to grasp: church leadership is not resisting foundational challenges; rather, it is resisting the casuistry of accommodation that so significantly helped build up the Catholic community over the past 400 years.

The first case appeared in the document from the United States Catholic Conference (USCC) Administrative Board, 'The Many Faces of AIDS'.[4] Here a healthcare worker has urged a person who has tested positive for HIV 'to live a chaste life'. But the document adds, 'if it is obvious that a person will not act without bringing harm to others', then a healthcare professional could advise a form of conduct which minimizes harm. Presumably, the healthcare professional could recommend the use of prophylactics. This position reflected in many ways the same type of casuistry that was found in an important pastoral letter by Cleveland Bishop Anthony M. Pilla.[5]

The USCC solution invoked the principle of toleration. This was the same principle that the bishops invoked when dealing with nuclear deterrence. Thus, in a good casuistic move, the USCC appropriated the logic of another case and made an important distinction: they were opposed to the promotion or advocacy of condoms, but when faced with a person who could further spread the disease and whose conduct would not be altered, they tolerated the advice that the patient should use a condom to prevent the spread of the disease. This position allowed the bishops both to resolve the new case and to protect the material principle that sex is illicit outside of marriage. It

---

3 K. T. Kelly, 1998, *New Directions in Sexual Ethics: Moral Theology and the Challenge of AIDS*, London: Geoffrey Chapman; see also Richard Smith, 1994, *AIDS, Gays and the American Catholic Church*, Cleveland: The Pilgrim Press.

4 USCC Adminisstrative Board, 'The Many Faces of AIDS: A Gospel Response', *Origins* 17:28, 1987, pp. 482–9.

5 Anthony M. Pilla, 'Statement on Developing an Approach by the Church to AIDS Education', *Origins* 16, 1987, pp. 692–3.

was a typical casuistry of accommodation, the same one used on nuclear deterrence.

This time other bishops rebuffed the casuistry. Bishop after archbishop registered a double concern: first, the solution could be construed as approving or promoting illicit sexual activity and therefore could compromise Catholic teaching and confuse the faithful; and second, condoms do not work effectively enough.[6]

Alongside the USCC statement many theologians attempted a casuistry of accommodation that was designed precisely to anticipate the bishops' first concern of compromising Catholic teaching. These theologians invoked traditional methodological principles to address bishops' anxieties that existing material moral principles would be undermined or made confusing. For instance, in addressing the case of the healthcare worker, Charles Bouchard and the late James Pollock[7] presented a history of the principle of toleration to highlight how traditional the USCC statement was. Later, David Hollenbach made a similar argument from commonsense logic.[8] Then Michael Place, one of the principal writers of 'The Many Faces of AIDS', invoked the principle of toleration to demonstrate that the USCC statement did not jeopardize but protected the church teaching on the exclusivity of marital relations.[9]

I published a long essay on the principle of co-operation similarly supporting the USCC statement.[10] The Irish theologian Enda McDonagh also proposed a casuistry in a time of AIDS, again arguing that no one endorses or approves either illicit sex-

---

6 'Reaction to AIDS Statement', *Origins* 17:28, 1987, pp. 489–93; 'Continued Reaction to AIDS Statement', *Origins* 17:30, 1988, pp. 516–22; 'Cardinal Ratzinger's Letter on AIDS Document', *Origins* 18:8, 1988, pp. 117–21.

7 Charles Bouchard and James Pollock, 'Condoms and the Common Good', *Second Opinion* 12, 1989, pp. 98–106.

8 David Hollenbach, 'AIDS Education: The Moral Substance', *America* 157, 1987, pp. 493–4.

9 Michael Place, 'The Many Faces of AIDS', *America* 158, 1988, p. 141.

10 James Keenan, 'Prophylactics, Toleration and Co-operation: Contemporary Problems and Traditional Principles', *International Philosophical Quarterly* 28, 1988, pp. 201–5.

ual activity or the 'quick-fix approach' as it had been dubbed[11] (see Chapter 3). The Austrian moral theologian, Hans Rotter, has written along similar lines.[12] Later, the Italian ethicist, Guido Davanzo, proposed the law of graduality as another casuistic device which would allow for the provision of condom information without compromising existing church teaching.[13]

David Kelly looked not only at Catholic healthcare workers offering advice to those who are HIV-positive, but also at married couples where one spouse is HIV-positive, and discussed how the use of a condom in their context was preventive, not contraceptive.[14] James Drane looked at Thomas Aquinas' writings on the object of an action and again developed a casuistry of accommodation for the cases of both the patient and the spouse who are positive.[15] For married couples, Béla Somfai invoked the principle of double effect and Dennis Ryan subsequently endorsed this position.[16] I, too, argued for life-giving ways to interpret the law so as to protect both the law and people's lives.[17] John Tuohey, invoking *Humanae Vitae*, offered his assessment of protecting that teaching while still acknowledging the moral liceity of using prophylactics in a marriage where one spouse is HIV-positive.[18] Finally, Josef Fuchs reminded us of the importance of the principle of *epikeia*

---

11 Enda McDonagh, 'Theology in a Time of AIDS', *Irish Theological Quarterly* 60, 1994, pp. 81–99.

12 Hans Rotter, 'AIDS: Some Theological and Pastoral Considerations', *Theology Digest* 39, pp. 235–9.

13 Guido Davanzo, 1998, 'Aspetti Morale', Milan, pp. 114–30.

14 David Kelly, 1991, *Critical Care Ethics*, Kansas City: Sheed and Ward, pp. 204–9.

15 James Drane, 'Condoms, AIDS and Catholic Ethics', *Commonweal* 189, 1991, pp. 188–92.

16 Béla Somfai, 'AIDS, Condoms and the Church', *Compass*, November 1987, p. 44; Dennis Regan, 'Perspectives from Moral Theology', *Dossiers and Documents: The Pandemic of AIDS: A Response by the Confederation of Caritas International*, February 1988, pp. 58–67.

17 James Keenan, 'Living with HIV/AIDS', *The Tablet*, 3 June 1995, p. 701.

18 John Touhey, 'Methodology or Ideology: The Condom and a Consistent Sexual Ethic', *Louvain Studies* 15, 1990, pp. 53–69.

which helps us to do the casuistry of accommodation that moral theologians are called to develop.[19]

I have found very few theologians who differ significantly from the positions in this list. The philosopher Janet Smith argued that the use of the principle of toleration in 'The Many Faces of AIDS' was unclear.[20] Mark Johnson argued that David Kelly's use of double effect was incorrect.[21] Neither author subsequently argued that advising on the use of prophylactics was itself wrong: they simply questioned a particular application of a particular principle. Only one writer objected to such advising, and he argued simply that the advising was scandalous.[22] One wonders whether he thinks that the Church's positions on ectopic pregnancies, pain administration to dying patients, and artificial insemination by husbands are also scandalous.

Despite this consensus of moral theologians offering traditional research for a casuistry that protects long-standing teaching while accommodating the value of protecting those at risk from the virus, the bishops still feared that they could cause confusion and so wrote another letter on AIDS, entitled 'Called to Compassion'. While not negating 'The Many Faces of AIDS', the bishops resisted addressing any persons living positively who do not abstain from sexual activity.[23] Evidently they resisted entertaining the case because they feared undermining the long-standing material principle regarding illicit sexual activity.

In the new pastoral letter, the bishops raised their second concern, again the effectiveness of condoms. This objection appeared several times in two national Catholic newspapers, *Our Sunday Visitor* and the *National Catholic Register* which

---

19 Josef Fuchs, 'Epikie – Der parktizierte Vorbehalt', *Stimmen der Zeit* 214, 1996, pp. 749–50.

20 Janet Smith, 'The Many Faces of AIDS and the Toleration of the Lesser Evil', *International Review of Natural Family Planning* 12, 1988, pp. 1–15.

21 Mark Johnson, 'The Principle of Double Effect and Safe Sex in Marriage: Reflections on a Suggestion', *Linacre Quarterly* 60, 1993, pp. 82–9.

22 Joseph Howard, 'The Use of the Condom for Disease Prevention', *Linacre Quarterly* 63, 1996, pp. 26–30.

23 NCCB, 'Called to Compassion: A Response to the HIV/AIDS Crisis', *Origins* 19, 1989, pp. 421, 423–4.

published a series of essays claiming simply that condoms were not safe, employing such titles as 'Sex, Lies and Latex: Study Busts Condom Myth'.[24] There and elsewhere, Catholics cited a variety of studies about the effectiveness of condoms.[25] But what would happen if these claims were challenged?

In the past four years, dramatic studies have shown that condoms are effective. The Jesuit physician Jon Fuller presents at length three studies that demonstrate the dramatic effect that condom use has had in stemming the spread of HIV.[26] One study appeared in the *New England Journal of Medicine*; it included 124 couples in which only one partner was HIV-positive. Consistent use of condoms showed not one infection after a period of two years and an estimated 15,000 acts of intercourse. Studies in Uganda and Thailand showed that preventive programmes which urged abstinence and if not that, then condoms, showed dramatic drops in infection rates.

In sum, moral theologians provided a very modest traditional casuistry of accommodation to allay the bishops' first concern: confusing the faithful and compromising traditional principles.[27] They also provided substantial empirical data to address

---

24 Julie Hoffman, 'Bennett and Carey Rap Condom Plan', *National Catholic Register* 68, 31 May 1992, p. 1; Russell Shaw, 'Condom "Cure" Questioned by Top AIDS Researcher', *Our Sunday Visitor* 82, 23 January 1994, p. 3; Russell Shaw, 'The Great Condom Con', *Columbia* 74, June 1994, p. 5; Jean-Marie Guenois, 'Sex, Lies and Latex: Study Busts Condom Myth', *Our Sunday Visitor* 86, 2 November 1997, p. 21.

25 Beverly Sottile-Malona, 'Condoms and AIDS', *America*, 21 November 1991, pp. 317–19; New York Bishops, 'Statement on Public Schools' Condom Distribution', *Origins* 22, 1993, pp. 553–6.

26 Jon Fuller, 'AIDS Prevention: A Challenge to the Catholic Moral Tradition', *America* 175, 28 December 1996, pp. 13–20.

27 They did not question the concern about condom distribution in the schools without parental consent, which a variety of Christian spokespeople, including *Commonweal* magazine, attacked. Reed Jolley, 'The Condom War on Children', *Christianity Today* 38, 1994, p. 19; 'Statement on Public Schools' Condom Distribution', *Origins* 22, 1993, pp. 553–6; 'Condom Sense', *Commonweal* 118, 1991, pp. 499–500; Whether the programme is morally right is one question, but recent studies suggest that condom distribution in schools does not promote sexual promiscuity. See Lynda Richardson, 'Condoms in School Said Not to Affect Teen-Age Sex Rate', *The New York Times*, 30 September 1997, pp. A1, 33.

the second objection. Despite these moves, workers in Catholic healthcare facilities know that adoption of this casuistry can still result in considerable sanctions from many local chanceries.[28]

In order to get a sense of the bishops' resistance, I turn to the second case. In the document 'Called to Compassion', the bishops argued against needle exchange, using the same two arguments: first, that people might perceive the bishops condoning illicit moral activity; and second, that the programme is not effective.[29]

Regarding the concern about confusion, Jon Fuller has applied the principle of co-operation to the issue of needle exchange.[30] Through a casuistry of accommodation, he argues in favour of protecting the teaching that drug use is morally wrong, while at the same time providing an accommodation for the present crisis. Fuller's recent proposal prompted a strong editorial endorsement by *America* magazine as well as support from Richard McCormick. McCormick proposed some commonsense casuistry that again highlights the traditional accommodation of a case in the face of chaos. Invoking the case of drunk-driving and the possibility that someone drunk could compound their irresponsibility by driving, McCormick made a comparison to the needle exchange programme and wrote, 'We say, don't drive while drunk; let someone else drive. But supporting the designated driver doesn't mean we support overdrinking; it simply means that we don't want the irresponsibility doubled.'[31] Moral argument again

28 See Mireya Navarro, 'Ethics of Giving AIDS Advice Troubles Catholic Hospitals', *The New York Times*, 3 January 1993, pp. 1, 24; or 'Vatican Intervenes to Stop HIV Pack', *The Tablet*, 18 November 1995, p. 1489.

29 See also Joseph Doolin, 'The Trouble with Needle Exchange Programs', *The Boston Pilot*, 8 May 1998, p. 8; New Jersey Catholic Conference, 'Statement on the Establishment of a Demonstration Needle and Syringe Exchange Program in the New Jersey Department of Health', November 1993.

30 Jon Fuller, 'Needle Exchange: Saving Lives', *America* 179, 18–25 July 1998, pp. 8–11. See Peter Catalso, 'The Ethics of Needle Exchange Programs for Intravenous Drug Users', refuting the principles in the newsletter of the Pope John Center, 1997.

31 'Needle Exchange Saves Lives', *America* 179, 18–25 July 1998, p. 3.

distinguished through casuistry the principle being protected from the particular case being solved.

Regarding the empirical success of needle exchange programmes, two complementary sets of data are important: one on HIV prevention; the other on the non-increase of drug use in light of needle exchange. In 1995, an advisory panel of the National Research Council and the Institute of Medicine declared that 'well-implemented needle-exchange programs can be effective in preventing the spread of HIV and do not increase the use of illegal drugs'.[32] Studies by the National Academy of Sciences, the General Accounting Office, the Centers for Disease Control and the University of California at Berkeley all found that needle-exchange programmes substantially lowered the spread of HIV and led to no increase in new drug use.[33] The programmes are backed by the AMA (American Medical Association) and the United States Conference of Mayors[34] as well as the National Institutes of Health.[35] Outside of the United States, similar reports of success come from many diverse studies, from Glasgow[36] to New Zealand.[37]

These programmes could have significant impact: preventing disease, illness and deaths. Instead the federal government continues to refuse to fund these programmes and the American

---

32 Cited in Fuller, p. 10. See Jacques Normand, 1995, *Preventing HIV Transmission: The Role of Sterile Needles and Bleach*, Washington, DC: National Academy Press.

33 'Federal Funds for Clean Needles', *The New York Times*, 22 February 1997, p. 16.

34 Katherine Seelye, 'A.M.A. Backs Drug-User Needle Exchanges', *The New York Times*, 27 June 1997, p. 15. See also Lawrence Gostin, 'Prevention of HIV/AIDS and Other Blood-Borne Diseases Among Injection Drug Users', *JAMA* 277, 1 January 1997, pp. 53–62.

35 'NIH Panel: Politics Hurting Fight Against AIDS', *The Nation's Health*, March 1997, p. 5; Warren Leary, 'Panel Endorses Disputed Study of Hypodermic Needle Program', *The New York Times*, 15 December 1996, p. A41.

36 Martin Frischer, 'Direct Evaluation of Needle and Syringe Exchange Programmes', *The Lancet* 347, 16 March 1996, p. 768.

37 Bronwen Lichtenstein, 'Needle Exchange Programs: New Zealand's Experience', *The American Journal of Public Health* 86, September 1996, p. 1319.

bishops' opposition to needle-exchange programmes remains unchanged. This failure to endorse needle-exchange programmes has caused scandal. In the British medical journal *The Lancet*, Peter Lurie claims that up to 9,666 HIV infections would have been prevented by needle-exchange programmes and adds that 'if current US policies are not changed . . . an additional 5,150–11,329 preventable HIV infections could occur by the year 2000'.[38] This year *The Lancet* wrote an editorial urging the Clinton administration to lift the ban against federal funding of these programmes. They noted that the US remains one of the few industrial countries that refuses to provide access to clean needles and that injection drug misuse is now the leading primary cause of paediatric AIDS.[39]

In comparing these two AIDS cases of condom use and needle exchange, I have made a traditional case to endorse these programmes without undermining traditional teachings. I think my argument is compelling. But these two cases do not help us to understand why the American bishops have failed to find them compelling even when they have both the traditional ethical structures as well as the hard empirical data that should allay their concerns and allow them to confront the cases before them in a constructive way.

In order to suggest a reason for the bishops' resistance, I turn to Jonsen and Toulmin's casuistic insight that stringing several cases together may allow us to see emerging congruencies. For this reason, I offer a third case. This concerns the fact that 12 years ago many religious orders in the United States, among them the Jesuits, began requiring that applicants to these orders submit to the HIV test as a condition for application.

Though the topic cannot be adequately treated here,[40] this

---

38 Peter Lurie, 'An Opportunity Lost: HIV Infections Associated with Lack of a National Needle-Exchange Programme in the USA', *The Lancet* 349, 1 March 1997, pp. 604–8.

39 'Needle-Exchange Programmes in the USA: Time to Act Now', *The Lancet* 351, 10 January 1998, p. 75.

40 Jack Anderson, 'How Healthy is Healthy Enough? Canon Law Considerations in Matters of Health and HIV–AIDS Testing Policies', *Horizon*, Winter 1993, pp. 8–18; R. R. Calvo, 1991, 'Admission to the Seminary and HIV Testing', *Roman Replies and CLS Advisory Opinions*

policy, perhaps not familiar to many, is an extraordinary one
inasmuch as, among all institutions in the US only religious
communities, the military and the prison system are permitted
by United States' law to require testing for HIV. While the US
Government can require such testing of those in prison and
in the military because their civil rights are already curtailed,
separation of Church and State allows religious orders to pursue an admissions policy at variance with the practices of every
other institution in the United States. Not only does this policy
reject many ethical and canonical considerations, it also contra-
dicts the USCC position in 'The Many Faces of AIDS' which
stated that 'We oppose the use of HIV antibody testing for
strictly discriminatory purposes.'[41]

The requirement for testing sets the stage, I think, for asking
what type of ethical reflection religious superiors engage in
when they initiate new protocols, especially ones that seem to
go against the standard ethical norms that govern society at
large. Concretely, what type of inquiry did the American Jesuit
provincials make when they installed this policy? And now, 12
years later, after dramatic advances have been made and people
are successfully 'living with HIV' and 'living with AIDS', what
structure do they have in place to revisit and possibly revise
these policies?

1991, Washington, DC: Canon Law Society of America, pp. 72–5; Jon
Fuller, 1994, 'HIV/AIDS: An Overview' in *Clergy and Religious and the
AIDS Epidemic*, Chicago: National Federation of Priests' Councils, pp. 3–
50, esp. pp. 27–9; Fuller, 'HIV – Considerations for Religious Orders and
Dioceses' in *Clergy and Religious*, pp. 57–76, esp. pp. 66–74; R. Gibbons,
'Admission to the Seminary and HIV Testing', *Roman Replies*, pp. 76–7;
James Keenan, 'HIV Testing of Seminary and Religious-Order Candidates',
Review for Religious 55, 1996, pp. 297–314; Keenan, 'The Return of
Casuistry', *Theological Studies* 57, 1996, pp. 123–9; Bill Kenkelen,
'Dilemma for Religious Orders: To Test or Not to Test for AIDS', *National
Catholic Reporter*, 9 February 1988; Jay O'Connor, 'HIV Testing of Appli-
cants', *Clergy and Religious*, pp. 77–82; James Schexnayder, 'HIV/AIDS
Policy Department', *Clergy and Religious*, pp. 83–6; Diocese of Oakland
HIV Policy Committee, 'Policy Statement', *Clergy and Religious*, pp. 87–93.
41 Administrative Board of the USCC, 'The Many Faces of AIDS: A
Gospel Response', *Origins* 17, 1987, pp. 482–9.

For several years I have been writing about these questions. It is not the issue itself that I find perplexing, however, but rather the way Jesuits, for instance, respond to the issue. Aside from the comments of scholastics who underwent the testing prior to their entrance, I have never heard any expression of interest in evaluating the policy. When the issue is raised, Jesuits simply attempt to justify the policy by their intuitions. They say things like, 'We require physical exams'; 'We are not an employer, we are a religious community'; 'We are a religious institute; applicants are not required to enter.' Granted these claims have some merit, there are other relevant issues. First, an HIV test is hardly like a physical exam. Besides, the obvious fact that physicals do not routinely include HIV testing, HIV testing represents a whole new approach to medicine. It does not describe a present pathology but rather forecasts the possibility of a future one. That is, HIV testing is like DNA testing that tries to predict one's future health. The fact that we use HIV testing means that we will probably require DNA testing for other health prognostications. Is this the type of screening that we want? Second, the prognosis for one who tests positive is strikingly different today from what it was ten years ago. Third, American society has made a powerful argument that one who is HIV-positive *lives* with it. Does our policy deny that claim? Fourth, if one were excluded from entrance for testing positive, what is it about being positive that is incongruent with our mission? Here the question of a purpose must be determined: is the protocol designed to satisfy insurance providers, to protect the superior from possibly more burdensome health issues, to insure that a candidate has a reasonably long life expectancy, to avoid the possibility of public scandal associated with a religious developing AIDS?

This resistance to ethically assess our policy highlights one basic concern: we want to keep the infection out of our ranks. I make this claim noting first that Catholic bishops, other church leaders and religious themselves have done and are doing a great deal in the service of people with HIV. Numerous cities have Catholic hospitals dedicated to treating people with HIV. Numerous Catholic agencies administer to their needs, and numerous religious work in supporting people with HIV. Since the beginning of the epidemic, in a variety of settings, Catholics have been among the first to minister to those suffering from the disease.

But 12 years ago, at the outset of our familiarity with AIDS, the religious were concerned about how the infection would affect their own members and their mission. Similarly, ten years ago when bishops reacted to 'The Many Faces of AIDS', they were concerned with whether preventive measures against the infection could in turn infect traditional principles on marriage, sex and drug use. Thus, when the three cases that I have proposed are put together, we see that both bishops and religious superiors betray an initial anxiety about the infection itself. Would AIDS infect the bishops' teachings and the religious' missions?

Several writers have noted the initial reluctance of many people to deal with HIV because it was a virus that struck, from our earlier perspective, the marginalized. In the initial familiarity with the disease, many thought of it as an avoidable infection that affected the avoidable: people with HIV were in Uganda or Haiti, in the Castro district of San Francisco or the Lower East Side of New York. Moreover, though the virus can be transmitted through various means, some of those infected were stigmatized as having engaged in immoral activity.[42] Shame was attached to this disease in a way that it has been attached to few others. Not surprisingly, shame was also attached to the preventive measures.[43]

Since we perceived the disease as mostly affecting those shamed by it who lived on the margins, our society thought less of prevention means for those endangered and more of protection for everyone else. Church leaders wanted to protect those living lives not infected by the conduct typically considered as the shameful conduit of the infection. Indeed, in AIDS' earliest

---

42 See Susan Sontag's classic 1989 work, *AIDS and Its Metaphors*, New York: Farrar, Straus and Giroux; William Rushing, 1995, *The AIDS Epidemic: Social Dimensions of an Infectious Disease*, Boulder: Westview Press; Robert Iles (ed.), 1989, *The Gospel Imperative in the Midst of AIDS*, Wilton, CO: Morehouse.

43 For instance, J. Michael McDermott, 'Is AIDS God's Punishment?', *Homiletic and Pastoral Review*, April 1991, pp. 32, 50–8.

stages, physicians and nurses wondered similarly how they could protect themselves and their institutions from the infection.

Eventually we have overcome our anxiety. Time, reasoning, reflection and experience have taught us to subdue our reactionary stances. Eventually we have realized that we can live in a time of AIDS and live with people who are HIV positive. The anxiety over the infection and its shame is abating. AIDS is becoming a disease like others, and effective methods of prevention for HIV are becoming as normative as effective methods of prevention for other diseases. We now realize we can live in a time of infection. Four reasons bear these claims out.

First, the original instinct of self-protection often precedes the instinct to work for prevention when an infection is at hand. Thus, the bishops understanding themselves as responsible for Catholic teaching sought to protect it in this time of threat. But, like the medical establishment that first sought to understand how to protect itself and its non-marginalized patients, church leaders too are now growing through this time of infection to begin considering the more chaotic questions of prevention.

Now, as we enter a second generation within a time of AIDS, Catholic leadership realizes that it both can be protective and advance the interests of prevention. For these reasons, we should expect to see Catholic leadership loosening its resistance and returning to its traditional ways of addressing cases while upholding existing principles. We have every reason to believe that in time, more bishops will not directly censure healthcare workers in Catholic facilities who in conscience recommend to their clients that they protect the common good, by abstinence, and, failing that, by prophylactic measures. Likewise, we should not expect the censure of moral theologians who assert the liceity of spouses protecting one another from their infection. And we can reasonably expect to see Catholic hospitals becoming progressively involved in needle exchange. Finally, some day (if not already) one of the American Jesuit provincials will accept a candidate who is HIV-positive, knowing that his illness is more a chronic condition than a terminal illness.

Second, several bishops around the world are turning to a casuistry of accommodation to address HIV preventive measures. In 1996, Bishop Rouet of the French Bishops' Social Commission issued a statement on AIDS which, through an appeal to the principle of the lesser evil, recognized the preventive function of the condom. This statement received a cautious but considered acceptance from many bishops, archbishops and cardinals around the world.[44] Similarly, the Rochester Catholic Family Center in New York has promoted the first US Catholic-supported needle-exchange programme. Moreover, as Jon Fuller reports, three Catholic agencies support extensive needle-exchange programmes throughout Australia. The state of Southern Australia alone has 55 exchange programmes for a population of only 1.2 million people. In that state, no new HIV infection has occurred from needle sharing in the last three years.

Third, these bishops are able to take these steps because the tradition provides them with a way, as I have attempted to show, both to protect existing principles and to simultaneously engage new problems creatively. We do not need to construct an entire new moral system, even at such a critical time as this one. Rather, the Catholic tradition is a supple and balanced legacy that we need to recognize, appreciate and utilize.

Finally, the tradition not only permits the bishops to engage these profoundly human issues, it urges them to do so. The tradition gave us the casuistry of accommodation, precisely because the tradition is animated at its best moments by the virtue of mercy. This virtue, which Thomas Aquinas considers

---

44 Craig Whitney, 'French Bishop Supports Some Use of Condoms to Prevent AIDS', *The New York Times*, 13 February 1996; Pamela Schaeffer, 'Condoms Tolerated to Avoid AIDS, French Bishops Say', *National Catholic Reporter*, 23 February 1996, p. 9; 'Caution Greets AIDS Statement by French Bishops', *The Tablet*, 24 February 1996, p. 272; Hubert Cornudet, 'AIDS and Humanity', *The Tablet*, 24 February 1996, pp. 256–7; 'Church Leaders Mix Condoms and Caveats', *National Catholic Reporter*, 15 March 1996. See also, 'Dutch Cardinal Says Condoms OK When Spouse Has AIDS', *Catholic News Service*, 16 February 1996; 'Vienna Archbishop Says Condoms Morally Acceptable to Fight AIDS', *Catholic News Service*, 3 April 1996. See also, Robert Vitillo, 'HIV/AIDS Prevention Education: A Special Concern for the Church', presentation for discussion at Caritas Internationalis, CAFOD Theological Consultation on HIV/AIDS, Pretoria, South Africa, 14 April 1998.

the one which likens us to God by imitating God's work,[45] is the willingness to enter into another's chaos. It is the virtue that appears in the case of the Good Samaritan who was called neighbour because he practised mercy. The Samaritan entered into the chaos of the wounded man lying on the margins of his society. But it was Venerable Bede among others who recognized in the case of the Samaritan the story of Jesus Christ. For Jesus is the Samaritan who in becoming human for us discovered Adam outside the Garden of Eden, wounded by sin and shame. Jesus tended to his wounds and carried him to the inn, which Bede realized was the Church where Jesus gave his life, our ransom, for our health or salvation. And still he promised that he would return and pay whatever debt remained outstanding.

In the Incarnation Jesus gave to the Church the possibility of practising mercy. This virtue, associated with being neighbourly to those suffering from illness and shame, ought to and does urge us to enter now into the chaos of AIDS.[46]

---

45 Thomas Aquinas, *Summa Theologica*, II.II.30.4.Ad3.

46 Roger Burggraeve, 'Une éthique de miséricorde', *Lumen Vitae* 49, 1994, pp. 281–96. I want to thank Jon Fuller, Tom Massaro and Robert McCleary for the many helpful comments they shared with me as I wrote this chapter.

Index of Names and Subjects

Index of Bible References